NO REPRESENTATION WITHOUT CONSULTATION

No Representation Without Consultation

a citizens' guide to Participatory Democracy

---

by PATRIZIA NANZ and CLAUS LEGGEWIE

Translated by DAMIAN HARRISON with STEPHEN ROCHE

BETWEEN THE LINES
TORONTO

Originally published in German in 2016 by Verlag Klaus Wagenbach (Berlin) as:
Die Konsultative: Mehr Demokratie durch Bürgerbeteiligung

First published in English in 2019 by
Between the Lines
401 Richmond Street West
Studio 281
Toronto, Ontario M5V 3A8
Canada
1-800-718-7201
www.btlbooks.com

Library and Archives Canada Cataloguing in Publication

Nanz, Patrizia
[Konsultative. English]
    No representation without consultation : a citizen's guide to
participatory democracy / by Patrizia Nanz and Claus Leggewie
; translated by Damian Harrison with Stephen Roche.

Translation of: Die Konsultative : mehr Demokratie durch
    Bürgerbeteiligung.
Includes bibliographical references and index.
Issued in print and electronic formats.
ISBN 978-1-77113-407-1 (softcover).--ISBN 978-1-77113-408-8
(EPUB).--ISBN 978-1-77113-409-5 (PDF)

    1. Political participation. 2. Democracy. I. Leggewie,
Claus, 1950-, author II. Harrison, Damian, translator
III. Roche, Stephen, translator IV. Title. V. Title: Konsultative.
English

JF799.N3613 2019   323'.042   C2018-906076-X
                                             C2018-906077-8

Text and cover design by Maggie Earle
Cover and interior illustrations by Christoph J. Kellner
Printed in Canada

 MIX
Paper from
responsible sources
FSC® C103567

We acknowledge the support of the Canada Council for the Arts. Nous remercions le Conseil des arts du Canada de son soutien. We acknowledge for their financial support of our publishing activities: the Government of Canada; and the Government of Ontario through the Ontario Arts Council, the Ontario Book Publishers Tax Credit program, and the Ontario Media Development Corporation.

Canada Council for the Arts   Conseil des Arts du Canada   Canada   ONTARIO ARTS COUNCIL / CONSEIL DES ARTS DE L'ONTARIO   ONTARIO CREATES

This book is dedicated to young activists around the world who are struggling to bring about a sustainable future for all.

TABLE OF CONTENTS

PREFACE TO THE ENGLISH EDITION

Much has changed in the world in the three years since we published the first German edition of this book, and sadly not for the better. Our proposal for the establishment of a fourth branch of government—a consultative pillar in the form of a network of "future councils"—was well received in Germany by town mayors, local councils, members of parliament, and state governors, as well as some of Germany's highest-ranking political representatives. And yet during this period the political climate has deteriorated dramatically both globally and within the European Union, including Germany, which no longer appears immune to the temptations of nationalist-authoritarian thinking. Sadly, the goodwill that greeted our proposal has not resulted in greater willingness to experiment with democratic practice through, for example, the establishment of future councils. (While the statutes of many municipalities already provide for various forms of public participation, such as citizens' assemblies, these are often poorly designed and half-hearted affairs that lack political clout.)

Leading elected representatives, including the German president and German chancellor, have warned repeatedly of the threats faced by democracy today. Yet, like political actors at the local and state levels, they have proved reluctant to tread new ground. With our political leaders unwilling to respond to these threats, the erosion of democracy has instead become merely a topic for late-night talk shows and cable-news panel discussions. Television is setting the political agenda, and the champions and organizers of democratic experiments are, like modern-day Cassandras, side-lined.

Meanwhile, the far right rejoices as citizens lose confidence in their elected representatives and turn their backs on established political parties. As this loss of confidence in representative democracy as a form of government spreads around the world, democratic political actors increasingly lack the courage of their own convictions. With its sham displays of democracy and overtures to various despots, the far right is positioning itself as the guardian of a popular democracy that would stand above the rule of law in its bid to exclude minorities from society. Our much-vaunted open society will devour its offspring if we, the citizenry, fail to defend the fundamental rights and values of democracy and to safeguard civic values, social cohesion, and the public sphere (by, for example, combating the growth of fake news).

We refuse to resign ourselves to this current state of affairs. Instead, we will make our proposal even more forcefully. We hope that the pressure to expand the scope of democratic participation "from below" will meet with understanding "from above." The time has come to move beyond mere rhetoric and to establish genuine opportunities for public participation to strengthen representative democracy. The middle class must abandon its political apathy and once more take an active role in clubs, associations, political parties, and civil society organizations. Only strong support among citizens for an expansion of democratic practice will empower elected representatives to regain control of the political agenda and set long-term goals for which they can assume responsibility.

In our view, democratic countries across the European Union and beyond must address the challenge of reinvigorating democracy. This challenge provides an opportunity to inject democratic politics into the digital sphere, which has so far been dominated by an emergent electronic populism facilitated by large digital media platforms. This book draws primarily on European and German experiences with public consultation and participation, but we believe that our proposed model can be applied in diverse contexts and circumstances. We hope that this new English translation of our book will foster a transatlantic and global debate on participatory democracy.

Introduction

THE CONSULTATIVE AS A FOURTH BRANCH OF GOVERNMENT

Some of our readers will have experienced the environmental and anti-nuclear movements of the 1970s at first hand; others will know of them only from history books. Throughout that decade, a wave of protest against the building of nuclear power plants swept across Europe and North America. In West Germany, the protests of the 1970s and 1980s—often remembered as a "participatory revolution"[1]—were partially successful in their struggle against the civilian use of nuclear power. In Lower Saxony, for example, protests forced the state governor, Ernst Albrecht, to concede that the reprocessing of nuclear waste in his region was "not politically feasible." Protests also forced Franz Josef Strauss, Bavaria's famously bullish and ultra-conservative governor, to abandon plans for the construction of a reprocessing plant near the town of Wackersdorf. (One of his successors, Horst Seehofer, perhaps mindful of Strauss's failure, recently sought to forestall similar potential protests by changing the route of a high-voltage transmission line that was to have passed close to Wackersdorf as part of the German government's

Grid Development Plan.)[2] And in Wyhl in the state of Baden-Württemberg, hundreds of thousands of citizens protested until a court order eventually banned the construction of a nuclear power plant there. An article published in the German current-affairs magazine *Der Spiegel* under the headline "Popular Protest—The Fourth Estate" noted that events in Wyhl had "propelled into public consciousness a phenomenon that has been building across the country's regions in countless acts of resistance and popular agitation over recent years: the growing influence of citizen-led initiatives on decision-making processes in politics, public administration, and business."[3]

Popular protest as the "fourth estate"? Surely not! After all, the press in Western democracies has long been referred to as the fourth estate (an extension of the medieval concept of the three estates of the realm: the nobility, the clergy, and commoners). The press has fondly claimed this title for itself whenever journalists have succeeded in holding the powerful to account by uncovering political scandals or state secrets, a task more properly performed by parliament and the judiciary. The fourth-estate label does not imply that the press functions as a state or establishment power, a role it would wholly reject. Like the lobbyists, think tanks, and consultants who seek to steer or otherwise influence state institutions and are sometimes referred to collectively as the fifth estate, the press is a non-state actor.[4] Yet what the aforementioned headline acknowledged was the existence of a sovereign authority outside of the three traditional branches of government—that is, the people, as represented by a flourishing culture of citizen activism.

Typically, discussions of the separation of powers refer to just three branches of government: the legislature, the executive, and the judiciary. Their division into distinct areas of responsibility forms the central pillars of modern democracy. Any attempt by the executive, for example, to direct (or hamper) the work of judges and prosecutors violates the principle of the separation of powers. The same can be said of the symbiotic relationships forged occasionally between governing parties and ministerial bureaucracies. Yet in practice the interlinkages between the branches often blur the clear division of powers. In Germany, as in the United States and Canada, this horizontal separation of powers is also supplemented by the vertical division of powers under a federal system of government. And then there are the various institutions which operate as de facto branches of government, among them the central banks and intelligence agencies, as well as the supranational institutions of the European Union.

As a model of state governance, the principle of the separation of powers is intended to prevent the misuse of state power by installing a system of mutual checks and balances. The Enlightenment philosopher Montesquieu in his treatise *The Spirit of the Laws* (1748) declared, "Le pouvoir arrête le pouvoir" (Power curbs power).[5] This principle informs Article 20 (2) of the German constitution: "All state authority is derived from the people. It shall be exercised by the people through elections and other votes and through specific legislative, executive and judicial bodies."[6] Some constitutions establish an even stricter separation of powers, while others favour the explicit system of checks and balances preferred by US founder and fourth president James Madison or the fusion of powers proposed by the British constitutional theorist Walter Bagehot.

This book makes a case for the establishment of a fourth branch of state power—a consultative branch, or pillar (referred to hereafter simply as the consultative)—providing for broad, in-depth public consultation both prior and subsequent to existing legislative and decision-making processes. The creation of this participatory branch of government would, we believe, enhance the operation of political systems that often struggle to meet the expectations of the citizenry. The consultative would not be a form of extra-parliamentary opposition (as seen in the Wyhl example above), nor would it curtail the powers of the current branches of government. On the contrary, its establishment would strengthen parliaments, which have been placed under considerable pressure in recent years as their credibility wanes. The establishment of a consultative branch would also demonstrate to state bureaucracies that their social, economic, and cultural projects can bear fruit only if they work with citizens rather than ignoring or acting against the wishes of an informed public.

Political scientists and others have for some time pondered the relevance of parliaments in contemporary political practice. What powers do parliaments still have, they ask, in an age of political globalization dominated by informal political networks and strong executives? In one recent example, Norbert Lammert, the former president of Germany's federal parliament, quite rightly warned in 2015 that parliament should not ratify the Transatlantic Trade and Investment Partnership agreement between the United States and European Union since it "had not been involved in bringing it about, nor had it been able to propose alternatives."[7] And in fact the secrecy surrounding the negotiations leading to this agreement, which would have had significant implications for existing social, environmental, and consumer protection standards, undermined the claims to democratic legitimacy of the state actors involved.

In political practice, executive organs (that is, the ministerial bureaucracies operating under the aegis of prime ministers or presidents) working in concert with parliamentary majorities leave opposition parties in particular with little scope for action.[8] The German parliament, for one, is known as a working parliament rather than a forum for meaningful political debate. Major debates occur there only in connection with weightier ethical issues, such as abortion or assisted suicide, on which parties permit members to vote according to their conscience rather than toeing the party or government line. Yet climate change and the impacts of digitalization are equally significant issues. Indeed, the prevention of calamitous climate change and the safeguarding of privacy in the Digital Age are monumental challenges whose solutions will need more than merely symbolic, top-down policies that the legislative branch is expected to rubber-stamp (or reject out of hand). In a system in which even elected legislators are increasingly excluded from actual decision-making processes on key issues, how are ordinary citizens to have their say?

While civil society has become increasingly self-assured, opportunities for public participation in the discussion and resolution of critical public affairs are lacking. Yet the importance of public consultation has long been acknowledged in both the theory and experimental practice of deliberative democracy, which emphasizes public debate and consultation and combines elements of consensus decision-making with majority rule. The consultative proposal we outline in the following chapters draws on both this deliberative approach, which has risen to prominence since the 1990s, and the (closely related) participatory theory of democracy, which was widely debated in the 1970s and 1980s. Both these approaches seek to mitigate citizens' sense of estrangement from the political system and place limits on political representatives' monopoly of power. Both emphasize the intrinsic value of participation, communicating in a way that fosters understanding, and the power of democracy to promote social integration. Proponents of participation also argue that it results in more effective policymaking.

Yet our consultative model does not call into question the structures of representative democracy. It neither restricts the legislative autonomy of parliaments nor exerts undue influence on the executive and judiciary branches. Representative democracy, despite various failings for which it is rightly criticized, remains unmatched as a method for distilling the will of society and arriving at decisions. To paraphrase Winston Churchill, it is "the best of all bad forms of government." Yet in the absence of public consultation, representative democracy suffers.

The separation of powers has never been a matter of unbending dogma. Instead, it has served as a guiding principle that can be adapted to changing times. The establishment of a model of public consultation that is comprehensive, institutionalized, and obligatory would be of enormous benefit to modern parliaments and would promote a more future-oriented outlook across the three existing branches of government. The consultative would lack an imperative mandate, meaning that unlike a binding referendum (another means of measuring the public will) its decisions would not have the force of law. Despite this, it would have standing within the democratic system. The legislative and executive branches would be required to take its findings into consideration and not merely treat it as a meaningless nuisance to be appeased.

Consultation has long been part of representative democracy. Drawing on the tradition of classical antiquity, Wilhelm Hennis once described humans as creatures that are, by their nature, in need of counsel.[9] The term "consultation" derives from the Latin *consulere* (to ask for advice, to consult, to seek counsel) and *consultare* (to consult carefully, to ask for advice). The noun "consultation," from the Latin *consultatio* (meeting, inquiry), was originally understood to refer to a medical consultation. Over time, its meaning broadened to encompass seeking the expert advice of qualified professionals of all kinds. Political elites now increasingly consult experts through various policy development vehicles, which often muddy the clear divisions embodied in the separation-of-powers concept. Parliaments and government ministries acknowledge that they do not themselves know enough about important (and sometimes vital) issues, a circumstance that invites experts and interest groups to influence decision-making. A host of advisory councils of varying degrees of independence and permanence serve the executive branch especially. In Germany, the best known of these are the German Council of Economic Experts (the so-called Five Sages) and the German Ethics Council. Parliaments also hold expert hearings and convene commissions of inquiry.[10] Lobbyists, too, contribute their expertise to the legislative process—while simultaneously advancing the interests of their clients. This is particularly evident in the development of health law, to which lobbyists contribute significantly. And, of course, the boundary between policy advice (which identifies options for addressing problems) and communications consulting (which proposes how problems and the decisions of political elites should best be framed and presented) is a fluid one.

The gathering of policy advice from diverse sources is a ubiquitous aspect of modern parliamentary practice. But career politicians, officials, and experts rarely consult the "wisdom of crowds."[11] Most find it difficult to imagine that a large group of ordinary citizens—assuming it is composed of independent individuals and is able to reach a consensus by fair means—could be smarter than an individual expert or that collective knowledge can or should inform political action. In the Ancient Greek *polis,* or city-state, citizens gathered to discuss the proper course of action. Likewise, pre- and early-modern parliaments were places of deliberation in which reasoned argument moderated the majority principle. Modern career politicians use expert opinions to validate their own decision-making authority (a variant of Carl Schmitt's *Dezisionismus* or political voluntarism) in order to supplant democratic decision-making processes. Yet policy decisions on any substantive issue should always involve a consideration of the political and moral aspects of the issue, even when experts or others claim that there are no alternatives. Even seemingly objective decisions, like the setting of maximum levels for contaminants in food-stuffs, entail implicit and fundamental value judgments. In such cases, expert knowledge can be made compatible with democracy only through a process of reciprocal learning involving political actors, science, and society. Within this context, decision-makers must recognize local knowledge held by citizens as valid and of equal importance.

There is an urgent need to re-politicize the advisory process and to involve the democratic sovereign—namely, the citizenry. The inclusion of some form of public partic-ipation in the policymaking process has largely met with approval since the 1970s.[12] Generally speaking, public par-ticipation encompasses all those actions and practices un-dertaken voluntarily by citizens with the aim of influencing decision-making at various levels of the political-administra-tive system, including elections, petitions, demonstrations, and referendums.[13] In contrast to constitutionally prescribed and legally regulated forms of participation, such as pub-lic hearings conducted within the framework of regional planning processes, and the classical mechanisms of direct democracy, such as binding referendums or non-binding plebiscites, new and innovative forums for public participa-tion offer a dialog-based form of political participation. To ensure that decisions are both informed and focused on the common good, dialog-based participatory processes should underpin decision-making that employs direct democrat-ic measures. Well-known examples of this practice include the citizens' assembly and referendum on reforms to the

electoral system in British Columbia, Canada, in 2004 and
the establishment of the Citizens' Assembly in the Republic
of Ireland in 2016.

This desire to complement the classical separation of
powers with participatory processes reflects the spirit of our
age. A range of proposals is circulating in academic circles
and on the Internet, including a model of democratic government that spans six branches, with regional, monetary, and
consultative components.[14] Our proposal differs from proposals such as these. As noted previously, the model described
here does not entail an imperative mandate (that is, power
to make legally binding decisions) and therefore enhances or
extends rather than challenges the classical separation of powers. At the same time, it is a decentralized, bottom-up model
of significantly broader scope than most proposals.

In referring to the consultative branch (the network of
future councils we are proposing, along with other temporary forms of participation in specific planning processes or
decisions) as the "fourth power," we strive not to erode the
democratic separation of powers or indeed representative
democracy itself but to underpin them with the empathetic wisdom of the citizenry by means of a modern, decentralized solution. The consultative can, to a certain extent,
compensate for the shortcomings of established democratic
bodies. By providing a forum for the articulation of value
conflicts, future councils can offset the growing depoliticiza-
tion of party politics and prevent well-organized stakeholders from dominating decision-making that concerns key
issues affecting our future. The growing power exercised by
private investors in urban development springs to mind here

(together with the cronyism and corruption for which the construction industry is known). In addition, future councils can relieve pressure on overstretched political actors by sharing responsibility for long-term or high-risk decisions and by bringing to decision-making processes both the diversity of the councils' participants and their constructive, collective wisdom.[15] By facilitating cooperation between citizens, politicians, experts, and government agencies, future councils can significantly expand the scope for political action and strengthen democracy as a whole—but only if established political institutions are willing to grant citizens a meaningful role in addressing future challenges, engage in genuine dialog, and provide clear feedback in response to the public's input.

Naysayers often deny the existence of an untapped potential for participation. Yet while the growing sense that ordinary people lack any real ability to influence the decisions that affect their lives and shape their futures has created a divide between the political system and its citizens, opinion polls in Germany, for example, suggest that around three-quarters of the population wishes to have a greater say and to participate in citizen forums.[16] This clearly suggests the need to identify and establish suitable formats for civic engagement and participation.

In the following chapters, we outline our proposal for a well-functioning consultative branch of government: a multi-layered network of advisory councils, spanning the entire country (and beyond) from the municipal through to the state and federal levels and even the supranational level (the European Union, for example, in the case of Germany and other European democracies). The consultative branch would advise decision-makers and the legislative branch in depth and on an ongoing basis. In a certain sense, a nascent consultative already exists in current arrangements for public consultation and participation, and it is growing stronger. The future council model outlined in detail in the fourth chapter offers a concrete example of how it could be institutionalized and made permanent. The inclusion in future councils of participants from diverse social strata and generations is intended to anchor political responsibility more broadly within society and overcome the excessive focus on the present moment that characterizes contemporary politics and that Anthony Giddens has previously criticized as "presentism."[17] Our proposal aims to broaden the horizons of both political elites and citizens to encompass medium- and long-term challenges and give greater consideration to the future consequences of present-day decision-making by considering how these decisions will be judged by future generations. We hope this will allow us to anticipate the steps that must be taken if our children, grandchildren, and great-grandchildren are to inherit a world in which they enjoy the quality of life and opportunities that we consider both desirable and appropriate today.

Chapter One

POST-DEMOCRACY? EXPERIMENT WITH DEMOCRACY!

Originally articulated in response to the outsourcing of political decision-making to the corporations and special interests that dominate our economic system, the hypothesis of a Post-Democratic Age has become so inflated as to encompass a general critique of the Western model of democracy that is at once sweeping and trivial.[18] Unlike in Western Europe after 1945 or the southern and eastern European peripheries after 1990, there is little enthusiasm for democracy among intellectuals and social scientists today. This "democratic fatigue" is reflected in an intellectual weariness and a blasé post-liberal, post-Western attitude among Europeans.

Responding to this defeatism, we wish to reaffirm the efficacy of (representative) democracy and, aware of its more acute deficiencies, initiate an experiment with the aim of strengthening and stabilizing it. In the rise of populism, which gnaws away at representative democracy like a cancer, we recognize a symptom of the current crisis. And yet there is a grain of truth to the populist claim that political elites are somehow "out of touch with the common people." Our proposal seeks to mitigate the threat to democracy posed by this sense of alienation—not by stifling, redirecting, or disqualifying the political sentiments that give rise to populism but instead by harnessing them for genuine civic engagement to enrich and advance democracy.

A Democratic Deficit

On the one hand, to speak of "post-democracy" is wrong given that, both in Europe and globally, democracy has not (yet) experienced a general decline in approval. Between the end of the Cold War in the early 1990s and the early 2010s the world experienced, in fact, an unexpected boom in democracy as a form of government and a way of life,[19] spreading into even the most obstinate zone of resistance, the Arab-Islamic world. On the other hand, recent data published by Freedom House (an independent watchdog organization dedicated to spreading democracy) reveal a dramatic erosion of democratic norms in many countries around the world between 2010 and 2017.[20] The prefix "post" is also accurate to the extent that the unbridled power wielded by large corporations, which are accountable only to their shareholders, has colonized the parliamentary decision-making system, reducing it frequently to a mere facade.

The critique of capitalism at the heart of the post-democracy hypothesis, first articulated by Colin Crouch, seems not only accurate but also suggests that the parallel historical processes of "global capitalization" and democratization have now run their course.[21] The new prosperity of the middle classes in the Global South has not automatically led to an embrace of democratic systems; in some cases it has coincided with the adoption of a positive attitude to autocracy. And the claims made during and after the financial crisis of 2008—that certain banks were "too big to fail" and had to be rescued at all costs and that there was "no alternative" to the bailout deals presented to Greece and several other countries in the Eurozone—severely undermined the good standing of democratic politics, which by their very nature must always offer alternatives. When alternatives are either non-evident or non-existent, ever larger segments of the public will inevitably conclude that there is no point voting for or engaging with political parties. And who can blame them for thinking so?

Social inequality within long-established democracies has undermined both the appeal and persuasiveness of representation. In the United States, the organs of popular representation are de facto clubs of millionaires and billionaires, whose membership is chosen by the upper-middle class. Meanwhile, the lower third and certainly the lower fifth of income earners are increasingly turning their backs on the political system.[22] This trend has spilled over into the customarily more participatory electoral democracies of Europe. Two recent examples from Germany illustrate this point: In September 2015, barely one in ten eligible voters in the socially disadvantaged northern districts of Essen took part in the runoff round of the mayoral election (notably, this direct ballot had been introduced in an attempt to stimulate voter engagement); And one month later only slightly more than 40 percent of eligible voters turned out in the mayoral election in Cologne, despite a highly charged atmosphere following the attempted assassination of one of the candidates on the final day of the campaign. These two examples reflect the diminishing interest in electoral politics, which became increasingly notable between the late 1960s and mid-1990s, particularly among low-income and educationally disadvantaged segments of society.[23]

While the productive capacity of market economies remains largely undisputed, surveys show that levels of discontent have increased significantly in countries with social market economies—that is, those countries whose social policies temper free-market capitalism by promoting fair competition and a welfare state.[24] The erosion of the welfare state and the encroachments of the economic system have opened the eyes of citizens in liberal democracies to the fact that they live not only in capitalist market economies but also in capitalist societies in which economic affairs are no longer embedded within social interactions and lived experiences. Instead, the managerial logic of corporations and banks has subjugated both politics and various aspects of everyday life.[25] As a result, anti-capitalist sentiment, which the post-Cold War decline of radical socialist alternatives had once relegated to the sidelines, is on the rise and is increasingly finding expression in right-wing populist agitation for a nationalist and ethnically exclusive model of the welfare state.

The rise of populism shows that doubts about the legitimacy of democracy extend beyond intellectual circles. A pronounced antipathy to the "upper crust" exists at many levels of society. This sentiment is directed not so much against those who actually control the levers of the economy but against political elites or "the political class." In Germany, mainstream news media have recently become the targets of this antipathy and are regularly vilified by populists and their followers as the *Lügenpresse*, or "lying press" (a pejorative coined by the Nazis), echoing similar developments in the United States, the United Kingdom, Italy, and elsewhere.

Social media networks and digital communication technologies have of course played a significant role in both the flourishing and the erosion of democratic culture over the last decade. On the one hand, digitalization provides citizens with easy and broad access to information, and social media convey the impression that their views and actions are of consequence. The Internet and especially various Web 2.0 applications (which emphasize user-generated content, participatory culture, and ease of use) have greatly increased the transparency of political processes though such online initiatives as www.lobbycontrol.de in Germany, www.govtrack.us and @YourRepsOnGuns in the United States, www.theyworkforyou.com in the United Kingdom, and www.openaustralia.org.au in Australia. The Internet has enabled like-minded people to build networks and mobilize supporters (for example, the "Campact" movement in Germany, which campaigns both online and offline). On the other hand, the largely anonymous social networks of Web 2.0—together with depoliticized television programming, or pseudo-politicized, in the case of talk shows—distance citizens from the political sphere. With its focus on finding like-minded others, this form of media consumption creates "echo chambers" that reject or excoriate dissenting opinion and act as a barrier to collective learning. Instead, it provides fertile ground for electronic populism and all kinds of conspiracy theories.[26]

Understanding Populists

The "paranoid style in American politics" that historian Richard Hofstadter saw at work in the United States during the McCarthy Era appears to have gone global.[27] The resentment that underpins conspiracy theories is not an individual or isolated sentiment; instead, it combines a variety of aversions. Resentment-laden individuals become deeply absorbed in their own malaise. They neither seek to rectify an unpopular state of affairs nor to spark reform or revolution; rather, they find contentment in the toxic "exuberance of fundamental opposition," fuelled by a steady diet of randomly chosen facts and insights.[28] They gather on the streets and at far-right demonstrations—in cities like Dresden, Leipzig, and Chemnitz in Germany and Portland, Washington, and Charlottesville in the United States—where they target ethnic, religious, and sexual minorities.

Populist political entrepreneurs see such demonstrations as expressions of the vox populi, or the true democratic will of the people, that render parliamentary politics ridiculous. Unlike Leninist or fascist radical opposition movements, modern populist protest movements exploit the democratic process to their own ends. They build majorities with the aim of establishing a hybrid regime that combines elements of authoritarianism and democracy. Typical examples of this so-called competitive authoritarianism include Vladimir Putin's "guided democracy" in the Russian Federation, Recep Tayyip Erdoğan's Neo-Ottomanism in Turkey, and the "illiberal democracy" of Viktor Orbán in Hungary.[29] Yet populism need not be our fate. If we manage to understand its motives and criticisms of the political system, we might use them to democratize democracy in a manner similar to the participatory democracy called for (and often practiced) by the left-leaning popular protest movements of the period from the 1960s to the 1980s.

Originally the term "populism" referred to the leftist, anti-capitalist tendencies that emerged in the late nineteenth century in the United States and Russia. In the United States, American farmers protesting the excesses of unbridled "Gilded Age" capitalism formed the People's Party, or Populist Party, and campaigned for business regulations, affordable lending, the adoption of the silver standard, referendums, and farmer cooperatives. For a time, the party enjoyed such success that Democrats and Republicans alike could not afford to ignore it. The egalitarian spirit of populism gave expression to the needs of the "common people" vis-à-vis rich and powerful elites, and its effects were felt during the Progressive and New Deal Eras. The term "populism" was also used in late nineteenth-century Russia to refer to the social-revolutionary *Narodniki* (Narodniks) who, beginning in the 1860s, actively opposed both czarist autocracy and the prospect of a capitalist Westernization of Russia. In their view, the rural village commune was the embryo of a socialist and egalitarian society. In the twentieth century, this left-populism spilled over into Latin America and other regions in the so-called Third World. In such places, nationalist-populist movements opposed to "Yankee" domination and global capital have tended to hold leftist values. This seminal tradition is reflected in the politics of the current regimes in Venezuela and Bolivia.

Populism is defined by its antagonistic theme of "the people" versus the political and economic elite.[30] Part and parcel of this outlook is an anti-capitalist sentiment directed against liberal market economies and industrial modernity. Yet while populism, like Marxism, draws on aspects of class struggle, in populism the antagonism between capital and labour does not take centre stage, as it does in Marxism. The kind of class struggle represented by populists (in all their historical and contemporary varieties) is a misguided one. In place of the socio-structural and normative antagonisms between upper and lower classes, poor and rich, capital and labour, populists simply contrapose "the elite" versus "the people." From this perspective, the people form a unified whole, as if holding a common position against political elites (the "political class"), economic elites (the "fat cats" and "lobbyists"), and opinion-makers (the "lying press"). Often, populists internationalize class struggle, recasting it as the antagonism between the people and the elites of the globalized economy (and its attending supranational politics). This has long been the ideological linchpin of fascist movements and regimes, in which "the people" were defined primarily in ethnic-racial terms and in opposition to "international Jewry" and its particularities. The anti-capitalist aspect of fascism is directed against "rapacious capital" rather than capitalism itself. This helps to explain how populism shifted to the right in the twentieth century—from an ideology that promoted the expansion of democracy to one that stifles it. (It also helps explain how Donald Trump can cast himself as a populist, despite his enormous wealth.) As a result of this shift, populism is no longer a driving force of liberal democracy but a deadly threat to it.

The Bulgarian political scientist Ivan Krastev has identified a kernel of truth in the propaganda of the populists—namely, that elites have indeed turned their backs on the tedious business of deliberation and the transparent negotiation of compromises in parliaments.[31] Instead they have adopted the technocratic style that characterizes the politics of "there is no alternative"; as noted above, this type of politics is inherently indifferent to argument. Another shortcoming of this style of governing is its explicitly dispassionate character. By providing few other opportunities for the public to engage with politics passionately and proportionately, technocratic governance relegates political emotion to the populist camp.

Politics for the Future

The rise of populism exposes genuine problems within liberal democracies—namely, the loss of their abilities to control, regulate, and steer developments, especially in times of crisis. The idea of democracy can be distilled into a single statement: citizens should be able to make or at the very least indirectly control the decisions that affect them. Economic, cultural, and political globalization undermines this rule, and its effects break open the container that is the nation-state. As a result, sovereign states are increasingly subject to decisions made far away without their input or legitimation; at the same time, decisions made "here" affect populations in other parts of the world.

Citizens' lack of control over decisions affecting them also has a temporal dimension; decisions made today will affect people tomorrow. This is not fundamentally new. The fragile infrastructures, unresolved conflicts, accumulated debts, and other legacy issues of our societies have always placed obligations on future generations. For example, politicians who authorized the civilian use of atomic energy in the 1950s—without first providing for the safe disposal of nuclear waste—curtailed the freedom and options of future generations to a far greater degree than they admitted at the time.[32] Sustainable development—defined by the now-legendary Brundtland Report of 1987 as that which "meets the needs of the present without compromising the ability of future generations to meet their own needs"—has become a major intergenerational issue in recent years.[33] Sustainability concerns not only the constituencies currently inhabiting a national territory (toward which policy is typically geared) but also "extraneous constituencies" located elsewhere and in the future. We cannot know how future generations will wish to live or whether they will feel harmed by our actions. But we can imagine both. In democratic terms, sustainability is quite simply a matter of intergenerational justice, and justice in turn is the very basis of democracy.

Responsible policymaking must therefore try to minimize as far as possible the impact on and harm to future generations, not least of all to safeguard the future of the democratic process. "Generation" is the only temporal category applicable to the organization of societies. Generations are biosocial hybrids; within the biological generational relationship, grandparents, parents, children, and grandchildren form a kinship chain along which material and immaterial values are passed from one generation to the next, directly through personal interaction and indirectly via memories. The public dimension of these private transfers can be found in the redistribution of wealth through welfare and pension policies, which at times spark intergenerational conflicts.

The "futurization of politics"—a term that refers to the rhetorical and factual reorientation of policymaking and decision-making towards the future—calls for a broader perspective on intergenerational relationships. (Practical examples of this "futurization" include the balanced-budget amendment to the German constitution, international agreements to achieve radical reductions in greenhouse gas emissions, and any policies that are guided by "planetary boundaries," like the two-degrees limit to prevent dangerous climate change.) The futurization of politics calls for long-term thinking that considers the relationship between present and future generations. The children and adolescents of today represent this relationship on a symbolic level. The question is: Must this representation remain a symbolic one? Or can it, directly or indirectly, take on an actual and democratic form?

Modern democracies have shown they can expand the representation of hitherto unrecognized interests. The right to vote, for example, expanded from censitary suffrage (a system in which votes cast by eligible voters were not weighted equally but rather according to a voter's rank and wealth) through universal manhood suffrage to women's suffrage in the twentieth century. More recently, many jurisdictions have lowered the voting age to eighteen, and some have granted voting rights to permanent residents and other non-nationals, especially at the municipal level.

In order to establish justice between generations, we must both broaden our thinking to include the interests of future generations in our decision-making processes and develop and equip institutions within representative democracy that are capable of achieving this aim. Social scientists have proposed models that include constitutional amendments to safeguard the "rights of future generations," sustainability councils staffed by experts, and public assemblies that put future challenges on the political agenda. Governments might integrate these elements into their existing institutions, or they might need to create new ones. In some models, the exercise of the hypothetical will of future generations is delegated to proxies, such as ombudspersons or (in a variation on the idea of children's suffrage) the parents of the next generation. Other ways of institutionally anchoring the interests of posterity include the introduction of "youth quotas" (reserving a portion of parliamentary seats for young people) or setting up consultative institutions, such as future councils, and charging them with ensuring that other democratic organs of the state consider the needs and rights of future generations.

Drawing on some of these ideas, policymakers in some countries have shown a growing willingness to tackle the issue of intergenerational equity. In Germany, for example, the former Minister of Family Affairs, Senior Citizens, Women, and Youth, Manuela Schwesig, recently suggested that parents be granted proxy votes on behalf of minors for whom they are responsible.[34] This would be a less than satisfactory solution, however. As critics of an earlier similar initiative argued, granting parents proxy votes as a form of indirect youth suffrage would lead to an accumulation of voting power in the hands of parents, raising substantial constitutional issues. And why wouldn't parents use these votes to promote their own, current interests?[35] In Germany, one recent attempt to protect the interests of minors and future generations was the initiative for an Intergenerational Equity Law. Launched in 2006 with the backing of more than a hundred younger members of parliament from across the political spectrum, this legislative initiative sought to amend the German constitution through the adoption of a new article (Article 20b). It read, "In its actions, the state must observe the principle of sustainability and protect the interests of future generations." But a draft of the bill did not get through parliament's legal affairs committee, and the issue was not taken up again by later parliaments.

Around the world, advocates of intergenerational equity have suggested and in some cases implemented a variety of proposals, ranging from mere expressions of intent to the appointment of ombudspersons or the allocation of parliamentary seats to special representatives of the interests of future generations. Our proposal for the institutionalization of future councils is yet another such attempt to "democratize democracy" and a variant of this kind of "democratic experimentalism."[36]

Deliberation Done Right

Our proposed consultative model stands in the tradition of experimentation with deliberative democratic models. In academic discourse, deliberation (from the Latin *deliberatio,* meaning consideration, consultation, or discussion) is a technical term for argumentative forms of communication (as opposed to purely declarative and confrontational ones) in which the individual arrives at her conviction by weighing and evaluating arguments to determine their veracity. The term originated in jurisprudence in reference to the weighting of the factors that contribute to a verdict. From this basis Jürgen Habermas developed the notion that legitimate lawmaking is generated through the public deliberation of citizens. "Deliberative democracy" presents an ideal of political autonomy based on practical reasoning among citizens. This means that the plurality of competing interests does not get the last word and is not the sole perspective considered in deciding matters of public importance.[37]

This concept has become influential in intellectual debates about democracy in recent decades and has inspired numerous practical experiments, particularly in North America and Europe, including "deliberative polls"[38] and "21st Century Town Hall Meetings."[39] Democratic innovations of this kind have grown increasingly radical and are reshaping the body of theory from which they sprang. The evolution of democracy is thus unfolding not only in the theories of philosophers and political scientists but also in the practice of deliberative, participatory experimentation.[40]

Yet critics have disparaged deliberative democratic models on several grounds. One of the more sweeping criticisms of deliberative democratic practice pertains to its more output-oriented manifestations, in which weakly legitimated experts and representatives of various associations and lobbies rather than individual citizens are the ones contributing to policy dialogs. (These forms of deliberation are frequently favoured by state actors as a means to generate acceptance of otherwise unpopular measures and projects, depoliticize decision-making, or hide policy outcomes from the oversight of democratic institutions.) In practice, such disingenuous dialogs promote the interests of elites and establish a "counter-democracy."[41] More process-oriented forms of deliberation anchor their legitimacy in how decisions are made and who is involved in making them. Yet one weighty objection to these forms of deliberation is that the inclusion of civil society and the citizenry in the decision-making process would dull the political core of democracy—namely, the resolving of disputes through political competition and majority vote—by making consensus a prerequisite for rather than a goal of any outcomes.[42] Still others claim that deliberative politics overstate the role of individual rationality while neglecting empathy and the importance for democracy of the "we" experienced in living communities.[43]

While these objections are substantial, we believe that deliberative democracy is the antithesis of what John Stuart Mill called the "tyranny of the majority,"[44] under which the most popular standpoint brushes aside worthier arguments—a regular occurrence in democracies that allow powerful stakeholders to prolong conflicts indefinitely until a decision is made in their favour. The frustration many citizens feel about politics often derives from the experience of seeing manifestly better arguments dismissed without further exploration or justification.

The consultative is located on the margins of deliberative politics. Embracing the complex and often "dirty" reality of political life, it reflects a more pragmatic approach than the Habermasian model.[45] Unlike the greats of political philosophy, among them Edmund Burke and Jean-Jacques Rousseau, who likened the formation of political judgment in the public sphere to a concert performance, we hold that it is always a contentious process. Hannah Arendt, who shared this view, held that the reflective use of our faculty of judgment provides for "the greatest possible overview of all possible standpoints and viewpoints."[46] It is this faculty that allows the individual to mentally put themselves in the place of another and to see things from divergent points of view. Partisan opinions and interests bound to particular ways of thinking form the core of any political dispute. They can and should be teased out and turned to productive purposes as a final decision is made, as it always must be in politics.

Our proposal aims to tame the anti-political passions of contemporary populism and re-politicize democracy at its core by empowering citizens to engage in long-term thinking and assume responsibility for future generations. Only by fostering greater participation can we overcome psychological, socio-structural, and power-political barriers to conventional participation.

Chapter Two
THE BEST AND WORST OF PARTICIPATORY DEMOCRACY

Twenty or thirty years ago, calls for greater public participation would have encountered considerable skepticism; extending public participation might jeopardize the institutional balance of representative democracy, empower dilettantes and troublemakers, and, in a sense, call into question the dignity of the state. Rather, citizens were urged to follow convention. They should vote in greater numbers and join political parties but not go beyond that. The political mood has changed radically since then, giving rise to a "participatory revolution." The practices and processes of participatory democracy have moved our "spectator democracies," which effectively bar citizens from actively taking part in decision-making processes dominated by elites and experts, toward a more participatory model. Today, almost any public event will include calls for greater participation, though this is often little more than lip service. Yet given the steady decline of "conventional" forms of participation (such as voting), the hopes of representative democracies now rest indisputably on "unconventional" forms of participation.

The grounds for this pendulum swing lie in a decades-long process of societal transformation that is underpinned by three key trends: Citizens want to participate in public affairs more directly and expect to have opportunities to do so; They are (on average) more educated than previous generations; And they are more critical of the political system and its decision-making processes.[47] Contemporary society is also marked by increasing differentiation; lifestyles, attitudes, and values are becoming more diverse and the differences between social milieus greater. As a result, irrespective of the specific political issue, reaching agreement on what constitutes the best outcome for all has become ever more difficult. Previously well-established political camps have disintegrated. The influence of quasi-political organizations such as "conservative" churches and "progressive" unions has greatly diminished. And public opinion has grown increasingly fickle.

In the light of these developments many academics and political organizations alike have for decades favoured increasing public participation; it offers a means to reform democratic politics and enrich the knowledge and value bases of political decisions through the inclusion of actors and groups previously uninvolved in the political process. These champions of participation hope that innovative methods of opinion-forming and decision-making will breathe new life into democracy.

Below we explore the best and worst of contemporary forms of participatory democracy. At their worst, public participation processes lack transparency and clearly defined roles in decision-making processes; have no chance of affecting decisions because they lack any real influence or are brought in too late in the policymaking process; co-opt their convenors and citizen-participants to serve the interests of economic and political elites; mask rather than solve the problems they are designed to address; and apply a (cynical) veneer of democracy to undemocratic decision-making. At their best, public participation processes work toward clearly defined objectives; They define and transparently assign the roles and responsibilities of those involved and recognize their competence; They are inclusive (bringing everyone to the table) and fully transparent (putting everything on the table); They afford real scope for action and offer clear alternatives; They require professionalism and provide opportunities for feedback; And, last but not least, successful participation processes are formalized or institutionalized in the legislative and executive branches.

The Rise of Participation

Since the beginning of the participation revolution in the 1960s, three goals have driven demands for broader participation: emancipation, legitimacy, and effectiveness.[48] In the 1960s, when large sections of the population in Western Europe and North America protested against the shortcomings of the democratic system and demanded a greater and more active role in the decisions that shaped their lives, the primary goal was emancipation. This was driven in part by a change in values—a shift away from the accumulation of material wealth toward goals such as self-realization and nature conservation.[49] The protests and demands for participation of various social movements, among them the civil rights, women's, student, peace, and environmental movements, challenged the authority of elected representatives. Eventually, their demands shifted the discourse of political participation. It now entailed more than merely voting or joining and actively supporting a political party or public association and extended to such goals as the co-management of public resources and infrastructure, transparent decision-making, social justice, the empowerment of underprivileged social groups, and the democratization of society as a whole.[50]

One example of far-reaching democratization based on principles of social justice is participatory budgeting, which was first tried by a political jurisdiction in Porto Alegre, Brazil, in the late 1980s. Since then, the citizens of this South Brazilian city have taken an active part in deciding how public money is spent. Neighbourhood committees throughout the city bring together as many people as possible to develop and discuss ideas for projects. A panel of representatives from these committees then collects proposals from across the city and prepares a shortlist. The panel then sends this list to both municipal authorities and elected officials who must take the proposals into account in their budgetary deliberations. Representatives from the respective committees supervise the projects that politicians and bureaucrats later adopt.

Of course, participatory budgeting has not been a panacea for all the city's ills. But the adoption of this intensive form of public participation has led to a decline in corruption in Porto Alegre and many other cities around the globe that have applied similar processes, while empowering citizens and boosting public confidence in democracy.[51] The enthusiastic involvement of poorer and educationally disadvantaged segments of the population in participatory budgeting is particularly noteworthy.[52] The process has thus provided an important counterweight to dominant special interests[53] and has functioned as a "school" of civic competence.[54]

The participation revolution has at times stalled since the 1960s. Yet marked progress has been made both within member states of the Organisation for Economic Co-Operation and Development and in emerging market economies (for example, in Brazil and India) since the United Nations' 1992 Rio Earth Summit and its Agenda 21 action plan, which called for local governments to adopt pathways to sustainable development. Agenda 21 spurred experiments with community-based governance and efforts to encourage closer dialog between political systems and citizens. By 2004, over 10,000 municipalities around the world had voluntarily adopted a "Local Agenda 21," though mandatory measures seldom featured in these programs. Such efforts, encompassing a variety of innovative approaches to opinion-forming and decision-making, have become increasingly common since the 1990s. They include local initiatives to promote civic engagement in disadvantaged neighbourhoods in European and North American cities; administrative reforms in Christchurch, New Zealand, and Kerala, India; and recent Irish and Icelandic constitutional conventions composed of randomly selected citizen-participants.

Since the 1990s, the participatory revolution has evolved beyond the protests and emancipatory demands typical of the popular movements that emerged in the 1960s. In many municipalities, cities, and regions, participation has become an organized and often self-evident practice that enhances the legitimacy of political decision-making by involving citizens and/or civil society organizations.[55] Yet in many cases participation remains an informal or non-institutionalized practice that neither challenges the de facto supremacy of professional policymakers and administrators nor alters the structure of the political system. In some cases it means merely creating opportunities for citizens to revise decisions rather than actually participate in making them.[56] But generally the goal is to make decision-making processes fairer and more transparent through public participation. The Association of German Cities notes that "legitimacy has become 'discursive' and is frequently only achieved through persuasion and negotiation." It recommends that local governments actively cultivate and engage with a culture of local public participation and planning.[57]

Although public participation has often been criticized as a hindrance to swift decision-making (there is some evidence for this), well-organized participatory processes can improve the efficacy of decision-making so that both the processes and their outcomes are viewed in a more positive light. This applies in particular to processes that (a) are facilitated by an existing institution (thereby minimizing start-up costs), (b) are well moderated, (c) take place within a reasonable timeframe, (d) contribute directly to decision-making, and (e) are, not least of all, genuinely representative and inclusive. While fulfilling these conditions can make decision-making processes more protracted, it also tends to improve them. Hasty decisions that lack political legitimacy and thus incite resistance have an infamous tendency to slow or even derail processes. So do legal challenges that drag on interminably. In recent years, government and business leaders have discovered in wider public participation a means to improve the effectiveness of decision-making by drawing on the knowledge and perspectives of a wide variety of actors. The Aarhus Convention on Access to Information, Public Participation in Decision-Making, and Access to Justice in Environmental Matters (1998),[58] which has been implemented in many European Union directives, reflects this focus on improving the efficacy of decision-making and on accessing the knowledge of local stakeholders.

While emancipation, legitimacy, and effectiveness remain key motivations for increasing participation, our proposal also focuses on another aspect of political participation: the initiation of social learning.[59] Participatory processes, particularly those that address future social, economic, and ecological challenges, can serve as a seedbed for shared learning experiences. Social learning reactivates the capacity of citizens and administrative and elected officials to engage constructively and profoundly with local issues that are connected to the "world outside"—namely, the global community, the ecosystem, and future generations. In an age of populist contempt for politics, social learning can rekindle political commitment.

While representative systems of government privilege the vote as the means of participation *par excellence*—as a consequence of which political elites often become isolated from public debate—participatory processes foster and facilitate social learning and thus broader public engagement in important discussions and the search for solutions. The degree of participation afforded citizens can vary from forums that merely seek their opinions on existing proposals to those that provide real opportunities for them to cooperate in designing proposals and (on rare occasions) to make decisions. Processes focused on fostering real dialog bring together citizens and political and administrative actors in the initial stages of decision-making. These often include several rounds of discussions and require the support of neutral moderators and experts from the scientific community and relevant professions. The purpose of such dialogs is to develop widely acceptable alternatives by gathering a variety of opinions and ultimately to find solutions that meet with the approval of almost everyone. In almost all cases the decision ultimately rests with a democratically legitimized representative institution, unlike in direct democratic processes such as referendums.

To date, a broad spectrum of dialog-focused participatory forums has been created in different places around the world. On one end of the spectrum are large-scale conventions, such as "21st Century Town Hall Meetings" with several thousand participants. On the other end are the "mini publics,"[60] usually small discursive forums, such as citizen councils, planning cells, and consensus conferences, that involve from ten to thirty citizens who represent a microcosm of public opinion.[61] Around twenty to thirty dialog-focused processes and methods are now used, supplemented by an increasing number of web-based approaches to participation.[62] These various formats differ in terms of their duration (from one day to several months), number of participants (from ten to several thousand), and method of selecting participants (self-selected, random, or targeted samplings of the population).

Each type of participatory forum and means of selecting participants has its advantages and disadvantages. The suitability of each depends on context and objectives. The planning cell, for example, is a useful tool for the development of energy-efficient measures at the community level, but it is less useful in resolving conflicts that may arise in relation to new transmission lines. The choice of format depends, in part, on the social and political views of those making the choice. For example, e-petitions and online platforms such as www.fixyourstreet.ie, which enables citizens in the Republic of Ireland to notify authorities of problems with public infrastructure (malfunctioning traffic lights and the like), reflect a functionalist notion of democracy, whereas participatory budgeting speaks to a more emancipatory vision.[63]

Different methods of selecting participants also have their advantages and disadvantages. Forums such as future workshops are, as a matter of principle, open to anyone interested in an issue, and participants make conscious decisions to engage in these participatory processes. Yet self-selection can create a "participatory elite," disproportionately composed of people with higher levels of formal education or more leisure time (such as students and retirees) and those enthusiasts who are sometimes derisively referred to as "the usual suspects" or "professional citizens." The random recruitment methods used in citizen councils and consensus conferences help to avoid such self-selection biases and also ensure certain interests do not dominate forums. Targeted approaches to recruitment (as practiced in mediation) enable organizers to invite particular individuals to ensure different interests are represented.

Recent decades have seen an encouraging trend toward the use of participatory processes at the local level in particular.[64] More and more elected officials are recognizing the benefits of working with interested citizens, as it grants them valuable insight into the needs and views of different segments of the population, helps them identify potential stumbling blocks at an early stage of decision-making, and ultimately improves the quality of the resulting policies. Our proposal builds on this momentum to establish participatory practices at the national and supranational levels.

Participatory Democracy in Germany

The state of participation initiatives in Germany today illustrates some of the strengths and weakness of current experiments in participatory democracy. As political scientist Winfried Thaa notes, "the growing politicization of technical and infrastructural projects by affected segments of the population" has contributed greatly to a crisis of representative democracy.[65] Public opposition to various infrastructure projects, many of them related to Germany's transition to a reliable and affordable low-carbon energy system,[66] has fuelled debate over this crisis and the need to address it through institutionalized forms of participation.

In the wake of the Fukushima Daiichi nuclear disaster in 2011, for example, Germany adopted ambitious goals for its transition toward sustainable energy, including the closure of all remaining nuclear power plants by 2022 and the reduction of the share of fossil-fuel sources in electricity production to a maximum of 20 percent. Yet conflict dogs efforts to develop and build the infrastructure necessary to make this a reality. To transport the wind power produced in the north and east of the country to its southern and western reaches, the existing power grid must be expanded through the construction of an added 3,500 kilometres of transmission lines. This expansion is widely viewed as the most critical bottleneck in the shift toward a sustainable energy system, and it clearly poses an enormous challenge technically, economically, socially, and culturally.[67] Crucially, it will touch the lives of many people. Some will find their neighbourhoods and communities changed by the proximity of new grid infrastructure. Others will see the value of their homes diminished and familiar landscapes transformed by the construction of pylons measuring up to one hundred meters in height.

Although most Germans support the transition to sustainable energy, many local residents, citizen-led initiatives, municipalities, and occasionally even state representatives (such as the former governor of Bavaria, Horst Seehofer) reject the current plans for the expansion of the power grid. The protests are already causing considerable delays. As is often the case with controversial infrastructure projects, the classical democratic process has left society at an impasse. Between them, the federal legislature, state governments, the federal grid regulator, and state-level planning authorities have been unable to lend these plans the required degree of legitimacy.

The lack of opportunity for meaningful participation in the decision-making and planning processes has fuelled public opposition and a wave of activism, leading to the establishment of grassroots initiatives that often enjoy the support of local councils, media, and even local mayors. Almost 90 percent of citizens want a greater say in the planning of infrastructure; one would struggle to find a politician in Germany who does not favour more participation or an infrastructure project that does not face demands for the same.[68] Opposing or ignoring citizens' concerns clearly raises the risk of failure. The question is: How can we create a public space for political deliberation that will foster a spirit of collective social responsibility and encourage citizens to move beyond NIMBYism, the "Not In My Backyard" attitude humorously referred to in Germany as the "Florian Principle" (in reference to an ironic prayer to Saint Florian, the patron saint of firefighters: "Oh Holy St. Florian, spare my house; set fire to another's")?[69] The existing legal framework for the planning of new grid infrastructure offers little scope for genuine participation, allowing only for informal participation around specific aspects (for example, public consultation on the routing of transmission lines). The growing number of dialog-focused participatory processes conducted in connection with the transition toward a sustainable energy system is thus by no means a sign of a strengthening of democracy, nor does it testify to a more emancipated public or a process of social learning in support of a societal transformation toward sustainability.

Mega-projects with such far-reaching consequences as those involved in Germany's energy transition need to be supported by high-quality public participation that address-es conflicts as they arise, fosters constructive debate, and delivers binding outcomes. The energy transition also calls for us to include such forms of participation at the start of the planning process rather than at the end, when they can only address questions related to implementation. But up to now, the inclusion of dialog-focused processes in the energy transition has not been mandatory, and there is no guaran-tee that their results will be considered in the planning of infrastructure projects. On the contrary, participation only occurs when a grid operator (a company or consortium of companies) agrees to it. Currently, public participation is all too often pursued for its own sake, resulting in little more than highly imaginative (yet wholly unrealistic) wish-lists that are destined to be buried in the filing cabinets and on the websites of administrative bodies.

In other areas of public policy, too, decision-makers of-ten initiate participatory processes merely to assuage public opposition to projects like the development of a new airport or the construction of a highway bypass or waste incinera-tion plant. Such processes do not offer any real room for maneuver because the key decisions have already been made or the results of the process are destined to be ignored. In these so-called feel-good or sham participation processes, the goal is to appear to embrace participation without actu-ally doing so. The non-binding and non-institutional char-acter of these processes also leaves them vulnerable to the whims of their conveners. While neutral and independent moderators can prevent certain individuals and groups from dominating the process, some mediators allow themselves to be co-opted in the pursuit of a pre-determined public relations goal and do not fulfill their role in an independent and professional manner.

In effective participation processes, well-defined and clearly communicated mandates and roles mitigate such risks, ensuring that all the involved parties are aware from the outset of the potential scope for action and how decision-makers will treat the results. But the inflationary and ineffective use of participatory processes often delivers little more than window dressing for political elites whose attempts to make compliant partners of angry citizens only heightens political disenchantment. This situation fosters rather than combats rising populism and creates a parody of civic participation, causing urban planner Klaus Selle to wonder, "Are we participating ourselves to death?"[70]

This cynicism toward participation has been fed by failed examples of participatory processes, like the mediation process launched to settle a dispute over Stuttgart 21, a major rail and urban development project. Stuttgart, the capital of the stolidly conservative German region of Swabia, is hardly a hotbed of political activism. Yet the project's proposed destruction of Stuttgart's city park and train station and its opaque planning process, which stifled debate and did not offer any real alternatives, outraged the city's more affluent citizens. The conflict was rooted in an antagonism between technical efficiency, on the one hand, and people's individual and collective sense of place, on the other. It revealed a cultural conflict over the priorities of urban development that party politics had not properly articulated or addressed.

The hastily arranged mediation process led by former federal minister Heiner Geissler ended up masking the conflict rather than resolving it. The process, broadcast on television, did bring together in talks for the first time various citizens' initiatives, politicians, and members of the board of Deutsche Bahn (Germany's semi-public rail company). But the parties involved were not invited to shape the process (for example, to determine whether its results would be binding or non-binding), it was conducted downstream from the democratic decision-making process, and it focused exclusively on technical issues, making it more of an exercise in fact-checking than mediation. While Geissler characterized the process that he led as an especially successful "experiment in democracy,"[71] its shambolic origins, improvised nature, and lack of meaningful consultation meant that it was anything but.[72]

Truly successful public participation reveals the various aspects of a problem or conflict, as well as the different principles and values that feed into it, enabling citizens to see beyond the depoliticizing narratives of party politics and allowing commonly held views to be called into question. Done properly, participation allows for an expression of a diversity of opinions; it taps into citizens' creativity in developing previously unimagined solutions. This is achieved by allowing people to contrast their views with those of others and to adjust their positions without necessarily abandoning them.

An urban development project in Bregenz, in the Voralberg region of Austria, offers a good example of this type of approach. In 2009, after several decades of political deadlock, the city finally put the finishing touches to a master plan to develop a large waterfront area. As always, the urban development process unfolded within a tightly controlled environment and was subject to many and often powerful interests and equally numerous regulatory constraints. But to ensure that it had the backing of citizens and to provide an avenue for their input during the planning phase, the city council convened a citizen council composed of randomly selected members. It soon became clear that from the citizens' point of view the legion of planners commissioned by the city had made a cardinal error. While none of the council participants held any relevant professional qualifications, they all recognized that the project offered a historic opportunity to bridge the divide between Lake Constance and the city of Bregenz, which were separated by a railway line and a busy road. The citizen council developed a variety of proposals, including one for a broad pedestrian overpass (dubbed the "Spanish Steps") that met with the unanimous approval of the city council. This example demonstrates the capacity of public participation to harness local knowledge in the interest of the common good. Rather than serving as the mouthpiece of a special interest group, the citizen council articulated the thinking of a broad and diverse (yet often silent) public about the future of the city.

Toward a New Culture of Participation

To date, most public participation processes are conducted on a selective, temporary basis and are not codified in law. Yet in Europe the prospects for the gradual institutionalization of public participation and the development of legal frameworks at the local and regional levels are promising. In Austria, the state of Vorarlberg has pioneered the institutionalization and broad implementation of public participation. In 1999, it established the Office for Future-Related Issues (OFRI) as an advisory unit that reports directly to the governor, or minister-president. The OFRI fosters political engagement on issues relating to sustainable development. To support this, the people of Vorarlberg have adopted a particular form of public participation—namely, wisdom councils. These councils allow administrative units to consult a sampling of citizens on important social issues at an early stage, giving them an overview of public opinion. The councils also develop policy recommendations for political decision-makers. In 2013, Vorarlberg's state constitution codified this broadening of representative democracy, enabling citizens to compel the state government to convene wisdom councils to discuss specific issues. This type of institutionalization provides a sense of permanency to the consultation process that fosters a culture of participation among citizens, business leaders, and politicians alike.

This precedent has inspired change elsewhere too. Germany has perhaps made the most progress toward the institutionalization of public participation, though so far only at the local and state levels. The city of Heidelberg, for example, has established a municipal coordination office for public participation.[73] The range of topics addressed by this office includes urban planning, land use, and climate protection; its mandate and activities are defined by the city's statutory guidelines for public consultation. The city also publishes on the Internet and well ahead of any deliberation by the local council a list of current planning proposals, enabling citizens to call for greater participation if they feel it is needed. Bonn and Leipzig have also developed guidelines for public participation and established coordination centres. And several other German cities have set up public participation structures for specific urban development projects. The "1,000 Ideas Project" in Mannheim, for example, made extensive use of public participation to guide the redevelopment of areas formerly occupied by military bases. The ideas gathered in these public consultations were collected in a white paper and submitted to the city council.[74] This process was coordinated by a newly established unit that cooperates with other municipal departments and is equipped with a staff of three and a dedicated budget. *Demoenergie*, a successful participation process that took place in Windischeschenbach, Bavaria, in connection with the development of new energy infrastructure, provides a promising model of public participation.[75] The respectful approach adopted by the initiators and facilitators of this process during the nine months of planning that preceded the participation phase laid the foundations for a culture of participation that was free of fear and mutual suspicion.

Institutionalizing public participation as these German cities have done would help to foster a culture of participation that brings together relevant actors before decisions are made, gives some permanency to participation processes, and safeguards the quality of public participation. This would create an environment in which actors can develop mutual trust irrespective of their conflicting interests and views.[76] Fair and trusting relationships are a prerequisite for open-ended processes in pursuit of outcomes that serve the public good to the highest possible degree. Policymakers, public officials, business representatives, and citizens must learn to listen to one another. Good public participation facilitates a constructive dialog that considers the different values and outlooks of all participants, many of which are too often ignored in discussions of technical matters. Deliberative public participation provides a space both for citizens to weigh up the pros and cons of different alternatives based on the premise that all points of view are worth considering and, ideally, to subsequently engage in collaborative decision-making.[77]

This calls for a radically different—and more politicized—approach to participation than that usually envisaged by public authorities and some scholars. In its classic form, deliberative public participation fulfills a purely advisory role, is conducted over clearly defined timescales, and is usually convened on an ad hoc basis. Many scholars have argued that to be successful deliberative formats must be conducted with small groups and, in many cases, behind closed doors. But such processes merely complement political institutions and societal structures without fundamentally changing them.

Whether processes such as those described above will suffice to resolve the crisis of representative democracy is an open question. In theory, participatory democracy offers a more radical perspective and advocates the broadest possible participation across as many issues as possible, with the goal of democratizing all aspects of politics and society.[78] It goes beyond formats that have a purely advisory function. Instead, it prefers forms of co-decision-making and co-governance (such as the participatory budgeting process adopted in Porto Alegre) that give citizens real power within democratic power structures. An increasing number of participatory forums provide opportunities not only for public consultation but also for collaborative development and planning, as seen, for example, in Bregenz (with the creation of the Spanish Steps) and in the *Demoenergie* project (which provides for co-planning of grid infrastructure).

The consultative model we propose in this book would create a sphere of institutionalized participation to ensure that decision-making processes consider citizens' fundamental beliefs and harness them for the public good. This sphere must be about how we shape our common future and is no place for vague promises. We must require the legislative and executive branches of democratic governments to make clear whether and to what extent the results of participatory consultations will contribute to the political process. This does not imply that the consultative ought to be given the same weight as the decision-making power of existing state institutions. Our point of reference here is Hannah Arendt's concept of the political sphere, which contrasts common action in public space with the actions of politicians, governments, or administrators. Arendt's theory emphasizes the political rationality that is manifest in communicative experiences and that transcends normal human relations. This dimension of (the ideal and continuously unfolding) political life is a reminder that it is our role as citizens to create this shared space for democratic self-determination.

The institutionalization of public participation is an essential step toward the establishment of a participatory democracy. This alone would give momentum to a broad process of social learning and mark a shift in the normative framework of collective action that has the potential to transform the political system. It will not be enough to merely add a thin facade of participation to a depoliticized democratic system. Rather, as we explain in the following chapter, what we need is a change in the very way in which democratic politics are conducted.

Chapter Three
ON THE SPIRIT OF COOPERATION

Public consultation can only be fruitful when all those involved bring a cooperative and trusting attitude to the table. Many critics will argue that this is an unrealistic and naive aspiration and that public consultation is vulnerable to the actions of spoilers who, by looking to maximize their gains at the expense of others, frustrate efforts to deliver an outcome that is beneficial to all. We understand that this is all too often precisely how the world works. Nevertheless, it is far from naive to entertain the possibility of other patterns of behaviour. Arguably, human beings possess a predisposition toward benevolent cooperation. Yet in the political realm unfavourable institutional arrangements often thwart cooperative tendencies. Developing the consultative branch of government would harness the cooperative potential of citizens. Our proposal for future councils would also allow us to cultivate a sense of empathy with future generations and thus inject principles of intergenerational justice into political decision-making.

Homo Cooperativus

Both philosophers and behavioural scientists suggest that the human ability to cooperate is capable of overriding self-interest and may even be innate. The predominance in human relations of self-serving actions does not disprove this vision of *homo cooperativus*—of people as beings that are capable of and indeed programmed for cooperation. *Homo cooperativus* and *homo economicus* (which envisions people as seeking to maximize personal gain) are heuristic designations that capture the complexity of human aspirations and actions. The ability to cooperate has evolved from the egoistic self-interest of the individual and has generally proven to be advantageous.[79] Even basic linguistic communication relies on cooperation—or more precisely, the cooperative interpretation of words in the context of their usage—to smooth the way for understanding. As game theory analyses have shown, cooperation is possible even among individuals who are motivated by egoistical, rational, and strategic considerations.[80]

"Pure" altruism is not a prerequisite for cooperation; an enlightened sense of self-interest suffices.[81] In other forms of social interaction, too, humans demonstrate this capacity for transcending the desire to maximize personal gain. Reciprocal gift-giving, for example, takes place even in the anarchic world of international relations.[82] Interdisciplinary research conducted at the Centre for Global Cooperation Research suggests that humans are well equipped to cooperate and can do so on the basis of rational consideration. Humans are potentially both selfish and altruistic and, most pertinently, can pursue complex and evolving endgames. Some experts have even suggested the existence of both "genetic altruism" and an innate human capacity for cooperation that is shaped by our sense of empathy.[83]

Empirical research on democracy, deliberation, and participation has, to date, placed too little emphasis on the conceptual and normative preconditions for achieving the common good in collective and political decision-making. In our view, empathy (understood as attentiveness and receptivity toward others) is more than a purely cognitive mode of understanding, as has long been assumed in political theory.[84] Recent philosophical inquiries have explored the status and dynamics of such emotions in politics. Martha Nussbaum, for example, has argued that it is love for their fellow citizens and homeland that motivates individuals to contribute to the continued existence and prosperity of society and to pursue particular notions of justice.[85] And according to Sharon Krause, reflecting on the feelings of others enables us to make better moral judgments.[86]

We are less concerned with the inclusion of emotions in politics than with a pluralistic broadening of the concept of political rationality. Our participatory initiative aims at overcoming the inherent reductionism of a notion of rationality that has, since the advent of modernity, banished interiority to the private sphere. Today, we are instrumental and rational in public life and empathetic and aesthetic beings only in private. Within the sphere of the political, too, we must overcome the antagonism between rationalism and romanticism, between external and internal values.[87] Here, we concur with the pragmatism of Jane Mansbridge who argues that cooperation and empathy underpin the democratic path to the common good: "Empathy can lead individuals to make another's good their own. Individual interests do not then overlap; instead, the separate individuals fuse, in a sense, into one."[88]

Yet the transformation of self-interest into common goals within a collective, empathic learning process does not require that individuals curb their interests; when the common good becomes a concern for individuals, they identify it as their own. The cooperative stewardship of common resources, defined by Nobel laureate Elinor Ostrom as the "commons," provides a useful analogy.[89] Richard Sennett supplies another, drawing on the example of a musical performance to offer a vivid illustration of the relationship between cooperation and empathy. In the course of a rehearsal, a cellist becomes aware that her colleagues are phrasing a sequence of a piece of music quite differently. An attentive musician, she acknowledges this difference. While the musicians may not eventually arrive at the same interpretation of the piece, they will become more aware of their respective points of view and will improve their understanding of each other. And from this open-ended exchange of ideas, the musicians gain both insight and pleasure without necessarily reconciling their differences. It is these "little dramas of deference and assertion" that make ensemble performances a pleasure.[90]

Cooperation and effective communication require an inquisitive mind and the ability to look beyond ourselves. They require neither uniformity of outlook nor that our views conform to those of others. Their great value is that they immunize us against gross simplifications and the fallacies of populism. In her essay "Truth and Politics," Hannah Arendt develops the idea of a mode of thinking that allows us to consider supposedly established facts from different subjective perspectives.[91] This ability to understand the diverse points of view from which a matter might be judged is, for Arendt, the essence of political thinking. Arendt calls on us all to engage in public debate on issues of common concern and sees in this the key to renewing our political world. In this sense, the true value of public participation, with its focus on dialog, lies in its ability to make visible contrasting world views and values concerning, for example, what constitutes a good life or the protection of the environment. Only in dialog—as opposed to argumentative discourse—can we take the individuality of the addressee into account.[92] Cooperation and the capacity for dialog in turn require empathy.

As modes of collective endeavour, cooperation and participation stand in contrast to the trends of privatization, individualization, and competition that are so common in contemporary society. Participation empowers and equips individuals as citizens to develop a common vision of their future. We place our hopes in the growing numbers of people engaging at a fundamental level with public and environmental issues, often out of concern for their future and that of their grandchildren.[93] The challenges faced by humankind are increasingly on a scale that cannot be adequately addressed by the individual. Instead, they call for the pooling of knowledge from diverse disciplines and perspectives. They require shared awareness of the issues at stake and a societal intelligence that only cooperation and participation can bring to light. Research conducted by Larry Leifer at the Stanford Center for Design Research and Alex Pentland at the Massachusetts Institute of Technology highlights the obsolescence of linear thinking in an age of complex, networked systems and shows that the capacity of the collective to solve problems is far superior to that of the individual.[94] We believe the disposition toward social cooperation that exists across broad sections of society should be further strengthened by developing an institutional framework that includes participatory processes that harness the human capacity for empathy, trust, and cooperation (or collaboration), as well as our desire for communal relationships.[95] Institutionalized public consultation, as proposed here, would foster the growth of this mindset.

Too often unfavourable institutional arrangements that foster short-term thinking and prioritize certain interests over others frustrate this predisposition to benevolent cooperation. Let us consider, for example, the immense problem of climate change, which threatens the future of the world as we know it. Given its enormous energy and resource footprints, the current fossil-fuel-led path of growth is a huge threat to future generations. Why then has the political response to this widely acknowledged issue been so feeble? In his seminal book *Why Cooperate?*, Scott Barrett argues that concerted efforts to prevent dangerous climate change are being hindered not so much by a lack of political will to coordinate climate protection but by an institutional structure that is inadequate to the task. The familiar linear process of analysis, planning, and implementation may be ill-suited to addressing these challenges.[96] And the solutions that we need will not be devised by some solitary genius, whether a gifted politician, business leader, public official, expert, or scientist.

Yet elected officials and representatives of political parties across the spectrum continue to engage in cyclical decision-making processes in an attempt to reach a compromise that will satisfy all interests—a practice that encourages political actors to prioritize short-term benefits and party interests during the current legislative period. They also tend to afford some interests more weight than others, often in the belief that alternatives are not available or that necessity compels them to do so. In discussions of how emissions might be reduced, they often defer to the short-term thinking of business and lobby groups who present themselves as the voice of the people. But this approach disregards the interests of future generations that climate change will inevitably affect.

Intergenerational Justice

Under these circumstances, the sweeping transformation of our economy and society that we so urgently need to fight climate change will not happen without broad public participation. Meeting our responsibilities to people in other parts of the world and to the planet will require the involvement of diverse citizens, experts, entrepreneurs, and politicians. If the exercise of our freedoms in the present is indeed limiting the possibilities of future generations, then we must take both intra- and intergenerational concerns into consideration in our decision-making. A precautionary approach to policymaking must consider both the limitations of our current knowledge and potentially negative future scenarios.

Such concerns have been neglected for decades in important matters like nuclear power and the storage of radioactive waste. Those who believed that experts could provide reliable guidance on safe levels of radiation exposure or the risks of nuclear waste repositories have since been proven wrong. If scientific truth is to fulfill all of the functions expected of it in relation to issues such as the storage of nuclear waste or climate protection, then it must be generated in a democratic and cooperative process of reciprocal learning involving not only scientists but also policymakers and various social actors. Achieving this will require that we overcome the systemic focus of policymaking on the present moment and consider the long-term consequences of our actions.

This "great transformation"[97] requires that we look beyond the familiar horizons of liberal democracy to consider our transnational responsibilities for the needs of our interdependent global society and our transgenerational responsibilities to future generations. More forward-looking, global thinking has played an increasingly important role in the fundamental philosophical debates of the last few years. The question is whether there is more to this than empty words and self-righteous rhetoric—that is, whether the scope of policymaking is really broadening to include previously "invisible" people.

To some extent, this shift is being made in many areas of policymaking. In climate protection and taxation, as well as environmental, social, health, and budgetary affairs, policymakers have adopted future-oriented goals (typically caps and other constraints such as balanced-budget provisions), setting specific dates in the not-too-distant future for their attainment. Examples of this practice can be found in climate change acts passed in the United Kingdom (2008), Mexico (2012), and Australia (2017). Other examples include the medium-term fiscal planning undertaken by Germany's federal and state governments, which have committed to balanced budgets into the 2020s, and the agreement in 2015 of the G7 (Group of Seven) states to reduce their emissions of greenhouse gases to zero by 2070, with equally ambitious interim targets and commitments. This admittedly vague orientation toward the future still lacks a particular nuance—that is, a retrospective view of the future (phrased in the future perfect tense) that focuses our minds on what we *will have achieved* by a specific point in the short- or medium-term.

We are thus particularly interested in the "surrogate representation" of future age cohorts, an issue that raises tough questions with respect to both theoretical and practical aspects of justice. Do we owe anything to future generations? If so, what is the extent of our responsibility? Would it suffice if we were to leave to future generations what we ourselves have enjoyed, or should we strive to give them a better life? Discussions of intergenerational justice tend to focus on the contemporary moment alone—that is, on the pursuit of justice for the younger, the middle-aged, and the older generations of today. The focus of policymaking must shift, however, from a focus on the distribution of resources among contemporary cohorts to their distribution across present and future generations. Intergenerational justice is thus understood as justice between past, present, and future generations. As Andreas Scherbel suggests, "In concrete terms, intergenerational justice means that both the youth of today and subsequent generations should enjoy the same opportunities in life as the generation currently exercising social and political responsibility."[98]

Some people believe that this focus on the rights of future generations places limits on their freedoms. Yet many parents go to great lengths to ensure that their children get a sound upbringing, can study at university, or inherit a mortgage-free house. This widespread willingness to forgo consumption in the present moment to safeguard and enhance the opportunities of future generations suggests that the notion of considering their interests is not entirely foreign to us. Such examples of intra-familial practice offer valuable insight into the more abstract relationship that exists between individuals and future generations. Our approach (and our hope) is that a consultative branch of government would serve, in a sense, as a political simulation of real-world communication between senior, middle-aged, and younger citizens. This approach is reflective of the intergenerational relationship that underpins families, in which members of three generations often live together or interact closely. This constellation of three generations forms the basis of a conversation focused on the future but in which the memories of older generations (including of moral catastrophes such as war) and "dialogs" with the legacies of past generations play a part.

We must also bear in mind that one generation passes infrastructure down to the next—from basic infrastructure such as drains, highways, and various urban systems to more controversial items such as temporary storage facilities for nuclear waste and (degraded) environmental systems. We also bequeath and inherit such complex threats to the Earth as climate change and the global biodiversity crisis. These, too, have been the subject of renewed interest in the ongoing conversation between the generations. In light of these interactions, we can safely assume that, in a certain sense, present generations routinely communicate with future generations in modern societies.

If distribution conflicts between young and old are not to hamstring future councils, their members will need to look beyond the immediate implications of our actions and instead focus on the relationship between future and current generations. We can anticipate the expectations of future generations by considering the circumstances that an individual now aged fifteen to thirty will face in the year 2070. If we are to achieve such far-reaching and distant goals as a complete elimination of greenhouse gas emissions, then we must consider their implications for and impact on the life of an individual in that age group. Technological developments alone will not deliver the necessary emissions reductions. Rather, such reductions will require massive changes in our way of life—across mobility, food systems, spatial planning and more.

It is our belief that the human aptitude for cooperation is much more developed than conventional political institutions assume. So how might we harness this capacity and instil it in institutional practices? How might we enhance cooperation within our democracy by creating public spheres that foster reflection across space and time? And how can society draw on the "wisdom of the many" and its capacity to examine issues from a multitude of perspectives and with greater regard to long-term consequences than any career politician can muster alone?[99]

If we are to achieve these goals, we will need to shift our focus from substantive matters (policies) to processes and procedures (politics); that is, we must consider how we wish to organize ourselves as a political community. The first step to this end will be to direct the growing willingness of citizens to engage with societal issues and political decision-making processes, encouraging a process of institutionalized re-politicization. We must also acknowledge the vital role of conscious interdependence (i.e. thinking in terms of the interconnected "we" rather than the individual "I") in the management of value conflicts and the pursuit of collective action.[100] Indeed, this is a prerequisite for successful social learning and the renewal—and the deepening or broadening—of any political community.[101] It requires that all those involved are genuinely willing to listen and withhold their judgment rather than assuming that they already know the answers. Innovative solutions can only emerge when we are prepared to tread new ground and acknowledge what we do not know. This, in turn, calls for participatory approaches and methods that harness our collective intelligence and build trusting relationships.[102] These approaches draw on the creativity of participants and provide a means for communities to grapple with even the most divisive issues.

Chapter Four
A PROPOSAL FOR FUTURE COUNCILS

The second chapter of this book reviewed the rich landscape of institutions and procedures of participatory democracy that constitutes a consultative or fourth branch of government, and the third argued for the need to institutionalize cooperative, participatory decision-making processes in order to achieve intergenerational justice and address serious issues affecting future generations. This brings us to the heart of our proposal—future councils. Although future councils can be set up at all decision-making levels from the local to the supranational, we envision local future councils as the core of the consultative. Future councils are (or will be) permanent bodies tasked with identifying important future problems and potential solutions. They would each consist of fifteen to twenty randomly selected persons (or forty to fifty, for national and supranational councils), providing for a representative sample of the population, especially with respect to its generational profile. The councils would meet regularly, and their members would receive a modest allowance to cover expenses during their two-year term of office. A team of administrative assistants with experience in facilitation would support the operation and management of the councils.[103]

While traditional citizen-led initiatives mobilize their supporters through street protests, petitions, and community meetings, participatory processes invite citizens to contribute their expertise and local knowledge to make individual planning processes more efficient and improve outcomes. The unique value of future councils lies in their capacity to explore issues more extensively than can be achieved through conferences, planning cells, or the like, which are temporary and convene for only a short period of time.[104] As permanent institutions future councils can address broader processes of transformation and complex medium- and long-term challenges that affect towns, nation-states, and regions over decades. They complement various other forms of civic engagement, self-organization, and participation, all of which would continue, of course, to play a role.

Our proposal draws on years of practical experience in the field of public participation,[105] during which we have repeatedly grappled with two issues in particular: how to better represent the interests of future generations through public participation; and how to identify the most critical future challenges among the plethora of problems facing humanity. Above all else, future councils offer a means to address the issue of intergenerational justice—a topic rarely addressed either in political theory or practice. Climate change, the ongoing decline in biodiversity, the global debt crisis, and recent worldwide migration trends have lent this issue concrete form, and it seems right that today's decision-making processes better consider the potential effects of these challenges on our children and grandchildren. Our proposal aims to ensure the compatibility of present-day decision-making with the interests of future generations.[106]

The creation of a network of future councils spanning the various levels of the political landscape—from the municipal to the regional, national, and supranational levels—may also help address challenges posed by the interaction of local and higher-level political institutions, as local realities collide with global structures and as we realize that many global problems can only be addressed at the local level. All politics may be local, as a cliché of American politics holds, but their effects are global. This expresses, in a nutshell, the *glocalization* of our world, or the merging of local and global concerns. The term *future council* encompasses both key aspects: institutionalization and a focus on the future. As with all things rooted in theory, the future council will need to prove its worth in practice. And to this end, we will now outline our proposal in more concrete terms.

Agendas

In the form proposed here, future councils provide a means to address long-term challenges and support projects (i.e. those with planning horizons of at least ten years) that are likely to affect future generations (including today's "under-twenties"), even where potential harms and conflicts of interest between generations are not yet clear. This approach counteracts the "presentism" that characterizes contemporary politics, in which actors always have their eyes on the next election, the latest poll, or a looming quarterly report.

There is no shortage of issues that future councils could address. These might include efforts to reduce private and public debt and the challenge of securing necessary investment in manufacturing and infrastructure in the face of high debt-servicing burdens; the transformation of business and society through the adoption of digital information and communication technologies (digitalization), which will have far-reaching consequences for employment, privacy, and politics; the preservation of common resources such as water; and the mitigation of major environmental threats such as climate change and species loss. Future councils could also address issues such as the complex demographic changes affecting many towns and cities because of aging— sometimes referred to as the Silver Tsunami—and recent influxes of refugees. The challenge of settling millions of refugees across Europe in decent conditions and easing their integration into mainstream society, for example, cannot be resolved in an ad hoc manner. Future councils would be well placed to discuss and supply advice on the suitability of sites for and the fair allocation of new housing; they could appraise urban planning proposals to ensure that new ghettos do not emerge and that rents remain affordable.

The unresolved problem of long-term nuclear waste management is another prominent issue that future councils could address. The prolonged toxic radioactivity of nuclear waste means it must be safely stored for decades or even centuries—time spans that far exceed human planning capacities. When Germany and other countries set up peaceful nuclear energy programs, parliaments only discussed the associated risks and precautions in the most superficial terms;

instead, politicians chose to rely on the advice of experts who, it soon became clear, were both biased and short-sighted in their recommendations.

This issue provides a particularly striking historical example of how the short-term decision-making processes of parliamentary majorities can affect future generations. Although the long-term problems associated with nuclear waste disposal eventually provoked protests and the mobilization of citizen-led initiatives on a scale seldom seen before, citizens were (and are) excluded from input into decisions on the issue due to the lack of any official forum for their input. But future councils could tackle this issue at all levels—from the local level where disposal sites are considered to the supranational level where organizations like the European Union deliberate on the issue in the context of a future European Energy Union. They would offer a concrete means by which citizens could move beyond a legitimate grievance—the desire to have nuclear waste dumps located anywhere but nearby—and assume responsibility for future generations. As Winfried Kretschmann, the Green Prime Minister of the state of Baden-Württemberg, succinctly observed: "We have to put the stuff somewhere."[107]

But one might ask, aren't these issues too abstract or too large for future councils to deal with? Isn't the scale of needed expertise beyond the abilities of ordinary citizens? The answer in both cases is "no." The very purpose of this form of participation is to address at the local level those large trends and mega-problems that ordinary citizens would otherwise feel disinclined to tackle. Consider, for example, the seventeen Sustainable Development Goals (and their associated 169 targets!) of the 2030 Agenda for Sustainable Development adopted by the United Nations in New York in September 2015. These goals include the abolition of poverty and hunger and the promotion of good health and well-being, quality education, gender equality, clean water and sanitation, affordable and clean energy, decent work and economic growth, sustainable and socially responsible industrialization, reduced inequalities, sustainable cities and communities, responsible consumption and production, comprehensive climate protection, marine conservation, biodiversity protection, peaceful societies, and a global partnership for sustainable development. Some of these goals are so broad that most people would find them worthy, at least until the issue of their implementation arises. Some of them may seem removed from the concerns of Europeans and North Americans. However, most of these issues hold opportunities for local action and could offer valuable insights for the work of a future council.[108]

Global agreements often rely on action at the local level. The 2015 Paris Climate Agreement is one such example. It aims to limit global warming to less than two degrees Celsius above pre-industrial levels and decarbonize the global economy to prevent dangerous climate change. These goals must be implemented through the adoption of sustainable modes of living that can only be developed and communicated not at the global level but at the local level, in countless places around the world.[109] This kind of local implementation of global agreements was precisely the aim of Local Agenda 21, which was adopted following the 1992 Earth Summit in Rio de Janeiro. Despite the shortcomings of its implementation in Germany (among them the failure to gain significant traction in many communities and a focus on highly specific near-term goals), many of the processes set up in this context are still functioning today. Indeed, Local Agenda 21 could serve to inspire future councils seeking to tackle global issues in alliances that bring together countries from the Global North and the Global South.[110] Future councils can and should place the global dimensions of issues they address on their agenda from the outset.

Harnessing the Wisdom of the Many

A future council is a knowledge-based institution, but not to the extent that it resembles a scientific seminar. Instead, a future council should be a lively affair that is representative of the diversity of public opinion and grants expression to quite different ideas about the future of our society. It should harness the creativity and wisdom of the many and facilitate social learning. Most people would reject outright the notion that local knowledge held by ordinary citizens is in some way "superior" to that of experts and would refer us to the various misguided and unfortunate decisions made through majority rule. But the democratic principle, which grants all citizens equal voting rights irrespective of their education or powers of judgment, is rooted in the very idea of the "wisdom of the crowd" as well as the rule of the majority.

Two quite different examples from Germany and Austria illustrate how citizen knowledge can contribute to political processes through public consultation and how institutionalized future councils could make even greater contributions. The first involves a program aimed at improving the energy efficiency and sustainability of existing residential buildings in the city of Bottrop in Germany's Ruhr region. When the refurbishment program, a local business initiative known as Innovation City Ruhr, was initially unveiled, apartment owners and tenants within the affected areas raised concerns about costs. The initiative responded by presenting case studies demonstrating how short-term investments in new heating and insulation systems would pay off in the medium term and even deliver returns over the long term; this "green solution" was cost-effective and would be supported by attractive financing options. Yet the targeted population (making up roughly 35 percent of households) remained skeptical. To determine the reason for this continued resistance researchers at the Essen-based Institute for Advanced Study in the Humanities implemented a multi-generational participation project. It revealed that their reluctance was driven by uncertainty as to whether and how these buildings might be used in the future, since current labour market forecasts suggested that fewer young people would remain in the region, leading to a decline in ownership and tenancies. In other words, the key issue was not financial or technical feasibility; rather, it was the prospect of looming demographic changes and the perceived need for employment and education initiatives that would prevent younger generations from leaving Bottrop. This is, of course, not the kind of challenge that a single, ad hoc citizen council can resolve. A future council, however, would be well suited to address such a long-term issue.[111]

Our second example addresses the pressing challenge of resettling and providing proper housing for large numbers of refugees and asylum-seekers in countries across Europe. In June 2015 in the Vorarlberg region of Austria, local authorities and the Office for Future-Related Issues,[112] which has organized citizen councils in the region for over a decade, convened an ad hoc citizen council to better understand both how politicians, civil society, and the general public might address this challenge and what people felt could be expected from these new arrivals. The results of these discussions have informed debate over these issues within the state government, the parliament, and communities across the province. The citizen council disseminated information to raise awareness of and sensitize the public to the issues involved, and it made concrete recommendations in support of efforts to identify suitable accommodations and settle newcomers. The European refugee crisis has shown that the knowledge and active support of the public and civil society organizations are indispensable to the delivery of a first response. But the long-term challenges presented by a changing population, growing interculturalism, and the need to develop appropriate social, educational, and economic policies to safeguard social cohesion within the region (a popular holiday destination in Austria) are topics more suited to consideration by a permanent future council than by the kind of pragmatic, "fire-brigade" response to humanitarian emergencies employed in this case.

Of course, to address such complex issues future council members will need to rely on more than just their common sense. They will need to access relevant knowledge and information resources. Planning expertise will be critical to addressing such issues as the transition to green energy and the identification of potential repositories for nuclear waste. As the *Demoenergie* participation process in Bavaria has shown, this need not be limited to conventional forms of one-way knowledge transfer in which knowledge passes from environmental and engineering experts to members of the public. Instead, experts can work with citizens to develop alternative solutions not previously envisaged.

Participant Selection

We expect that local initiatives from civil society and local government bodies will seek to establish future councils. Most likely, this will occur in areas where a culture of participation has already taken root or where a lack of civic engagement has resulted in a backlog of needed reforms. Once this model of participation has proven its worth in individual towns and communities, citizens elsewhere will soon take it upon themselves to start their own future councils. Forward-thinking municipal councils and administrative bodies might also be inspired to start future councils at the local level as an important and useful addition to their own work.

However they are started, future councils must be designed with a view to maintaining group cohesion, preventing the emergence of cliques, facilitating effective and fair communication, and promoting creative group processes. To achieve this, they should include no more than fifteen to twenty participants at the local level and forty to fifty participants at the state, federal, and supranational (e.g. European

Union) levels. Anthropological studies and group experiments have shown that social interactions of the kind desirable in future councils become dysfunctional when more than 150 people are involved. Within social groups including around twenty-five people, the members are able to develop diffuse yet relatively stable relationships.[113] In other words, group members know each other, if not especially well; they meet frequently and develop a group identity not based on kinship, friendship, or dependencies. In order to become true members of a group, people must develop a sense of belonging that is in turn actively affirmed by the group.

We suggest that future council members be chosen through an adjusted process of random selection. A future council made up solely of society's most active citizens would be far from representative, as would a council composed exclusively of citizens directly affected by the issues it considers. An adjusted random selection method eases the recruitment of individuals from groups often underrepresented in public participation, which men, lifelong citizens, high-income earners, and holders of higher formal qualifications tend to dominate. To function effectively, participatory democracy must be responsive to differences in the ability and willingness of individuals to engage in public life and also reflect the population's heterogeneous composition. Achieving an ideal composition may seem all but impossible. Lottery-based selection methods are one way of avoiding such distortions. These have been a feature of democratic practice since antiquity and have become increasingly popular in recent years.[114]

Better still would be an adjusted process of random selection[115] that ensures the fair and equal representation of all age groups, which is a primary concern. We propose that the minimum age for participation in a future council be fourteen, the age in Germany at which secondary pupils can take part in decision-making processes within their schools. (It has been suggested that the legal voting age should be lowered accordingly.)[116] Given the considerable number of retirees who willingly take part in public life, a maximum age limit should not be set. The gender balance of future councils is another key concern. Although women tend to be well-represented in unconventional forms of participation and especially in voluntary work, they continue to be underrepresented in the political sphere and within industry associations. It is equally important that future councils bring together citizens with different educational backgrounds and afford immigrants adequate representation. Where regional identities are still highly relevant, as they are in many countries including modern Germany (strong regional identities exist, for example, in Swabia, Baden, the Rhineland, Westphalia, Franconia, and Bavaria), care must also be taken to ensure adequate regional representation on future councils operating above the local level.[117] Even individual suburbs and neighbourhoods can develop their own (at times antagonistic) local identities, and these may need to be taken into account in the selection process too.

While this selection method may not be precisely statistically representative, it can generate a "minipopulus"[118] that is sufficiently representative to express the will of the citizenry. After all, future councils not only represent the citizenry, they must be representative of the citizenry.[119] Ideally, they should embody the diversity of a society and its thinking—not an abstract common good but rather the plurality of public opinion.[120] Obviously, it is impossible for a group of fifteen to twenty individuals to completely reflect the diversity and dynamics of society. However, drawing on a sufficiently large sample,[121] adjusted random recruitment procedures can produce heterogeneous groups and thus ensure that particular interests do not dominate the council.

The selection process that we propose is akin to a lottery. At the local level, organizers would draw on a sample of between five hundred and one thousand people sourced from relevant government databases (in Germany, the public register of residents) in compliance with any applicable privacy laws. Suitable candidates identified as part of the modified random selection process would then be invited to serve on the future council, and a hotline would be established to provide further information. If a candidate refuses this invitation, the size of the initial sample would allow organizers to identify and contact additional candidates using the criteria noted above (age, education, gender, migration background, and regional identity).

The empirical evidence suggests that only a fraction of the candidates identified using this method will agree to actively engage in such a participatory process. (In Vorarlberg, for example, where citizen councils are now well-established, the response rate to invitations to join the regional council is 4 percent.) We understand all too well that engaging in a process of this kind is a substantial commitment for any citizen to make. While polls suggest that around three-quarters of the German population "wishes to have a greater say and to participate in citizen forums," many would in fact be unable to take up the opportunity.

Modern democracies, it seems, continue to be dogged by the "iron law of oligarchy" formulated by the sociologist Robert Michels early last century—that is, better-educated demographic groups with more time on their hands are more likely to participate in public life. We anticipate that this phenomenon will also affect future councils, and care must therefore be taken to ensure that the pathways to participation do not favour those who are better able to balance the demands of professional, family, and civic commitments. In order to minimize this, communications should be tailored to disadvantaged or less educated (and possibly very young) citizens in order to encourage their participation. Citizenship should not be an inclusion criterion; newcomers are often a source of innovative thinking, and their involvement in public life fosters their integration into the community. Holders of permanent residency permits and asylum-seekers who have lived in a municipality for a minimum of one year should be eligible to serve on future councils.

In addition to these considerations, it is important that a broad mix of generational cohorts (i.e. persons under the age of thirty, between the ages of thirty and sixty, and over sixty) are represented on future councils if they are to act as forums for intergenerational dialog. Just as many older and younger people are choosing to cohabit in multigenerational homes so that they can support each other with the creativity, thinking, and experiences specific to their respective generations, we believe the collective wisdom of a single generation will not suffice to overcome many of the challenges that lie ahead of us. Improving members' awareness of different perspectives and experiences will be critical if the interests of future generations are to be adequately represented.[122] Experiments drawn from psychoanalytic practice, representing the different structural constellations of our societies, may also prove useful in this context. For example, a few chairs could be left vacant at council meetings as a reminder of the (likely) interests of future generations. Theatrical and narrative practices drawn from the performing arts can also be used to evoke a space of the imaginary and to foster deep thinking about alternative futures and the interests of those yet unborn.[123]

Of course, individual members may choose to resign from a council after attending just a few meetings. But the example set by lay judges and jurors in Germany suggests that many citizens are highly motivated and are even willing to prioritize their duties over leisure activities or during holiday periods. This is hardly surprising considering that they are chosen from a pool of candidates with a declared interest in civic service, a circumstance that facilitates cautious and informed decision-making, usually resulting in well-considered judgments. But this analogy has its limits in that lay judges are inclined to adopt a dispassionate view, whereas members of future councils are often directly affected by the issues at stake.

It will be important to develop mechanisms that enable people to serve on future councils over the longer term while also placing reasonable limits on the length of their service. Members of local councils should be encouraged to hold office for a period of at least one year, with the option of serving for another year before resigning, moving up to a regional future council, or temporarily suspending their membership.[124] In regions or countries where a large network of future councils exists, members who relocate during their term of office should be granted the option of serving on a future council in their new locality. And, of course, safeguards need to be developed to prevent clientelism and corruption. These could, for example, take the form of an anti-corruption pledge such as has become common in many private sector settings.

While serving on a future council is not a full-time occupation, the demands of this role certainly set it apart from a typical volunteer activity that citizens attend to in their spare time. Councillors will need to be highly motivated and able to forge empathic relationships with other members throughout their term of office. While opinion leaders will inevitably emerge in the course of council work, as will the notorious and stifling phenomenon of groupthink, the diverse composition of future councils will counteract their influence. Together, the members must strike a balance between their commitment to the public good and the need to develop convivial working relationships. The day-to-day business of the future council should be more a matter of work than of pleasure, but equally more one of inclination than of duty.

Operations

We recommend that small administrative teams support future councils at the local, state, and federal levels in their day-to-day operations. These teams, which would be tasked with planning and conducting council meetings, would ideally be composed of experts holding qualifications in professional facilitation and mediation, ensuring a strong focus on goal-oriented dialog and debate.[125] Like all civil servants, the administrative assistants will undoubtedly hold their own political views but will adopt a neutral stance in their professional dealings. The clear trend toward the professionalization of such roles reflects a growing interest in public participation among moderators, supervisors, judges, human resource managers, organizational consultants, and therapists.[126] In addition, relevant postgraduate and master's programs should be established at colleges and universities (see, for example, the Planning and Participation program at the University of Stuttgart),[127] and positions in these administrative teams should be ranked comparatively high on the civil service grade scale.

The administrative teams and moderators provide a supportive framework, safeguarding the quality of communications and enabling council members to organize their work processes independently. Together with the members of the future council, they develop work flows and identify suitable discussion methods, such as the Circle Method. This simple approach has been applied successfully in a variety of cultural settings. It promotes participation (including that of silent participants), consensus building, and a sense of responsibility. Moderators open each meeting with an introductory circle in which participants are invited to speak, for example, about their motives for participating. Moderators then conclude meetings with a closing circle in which participants reflect on what they learned from the council's deliberations.[128] The creative potential and focus on the common good that such well-executed participatory processes can unleash is quite astonishing, and many career politicians who have engaged with such processes find it to be an eye-opening experience.

Moderators support newly convened councils in their first sessions by explaining the rules of participation, highlighting key points when discussions stall, reining in overly enthusiastic speakers, mediating conflicts, encouraging more reticent participants to articulate their opinions, and, at the end of each session, summarizing the insights gained and issues outstanding and then thanking the participants. Moderators should aim to strengthen each group's self-sufficiency, ideally rendering themselves superfluous in the process. Discussions that touch on deeper value conflicts may require support in the form of ongoing supervision and more complex dialog methods.[129] In general, it's up to facilitators to show councils how they can both reach and strengthen a consensus and mobilize the council's diversity for the common good by acknowledging and nurturing the temperaments, talents, and qualities of participants.

Experience has shown that a heterogeneous mix of participants can boost the creativity and quality of outputs, particularly in smaller discussion groups, and a lot will depend on the roles that participants assume as the future council evolves. More reserved participants often make the most insightful or constructive contributions. Then there are the know-it-alls, the conversationalists who can paralyze a group with their chatter, and the saboteurs whose subconscious destructive impulses are soon frustrated by the participative methods employed at future council meetings. The presence of participants with a good sense of humour can help to create a relaxed atmosphere. In most groups, opinion leaders with an innate authority will also emerge, along with individuals who work on an emotional level to foster group cohesion. And finally, there are the "work horses" who toil through the night to draft documents and dig through files, and the spontaneous thinkers who are at their most productive when engaged in dialog. Guiding this diverse cast of participants toward a positive outcome is critical to the success of a future council.

The question of whether and precisely when moderators must take a step back or intervene to safeguard the success of months or (in some cases) years of work is a matter of intuition. However, they have a clear role to play in helping future councils visualize results and in documenting councils' findings and recommendations at the conclusion of their term of office. Moderators can also contribute by drafting and editing texts, focusing discussions, and, when necessary, setting less critical issues aside. Yet moderators must not intervene in discussions at a substantive level. Instead, their role is to monitor deliberations and ensure that all members are kept abreast of planning developments, schedules, and the progress of council work and relevant group dynamics. Moderators support the smooth operation of future councils, the members of which are not professionals but laypeople, not experts but self-confident amateurs equipped with a healthy measure of common sense.

Council moderators should also facilitate opportunities for future councils to engage with the wider public. For many people, the charm of future councils lies in their exclusion of career politicians and provision of a space for those commonly affected by politics but normally excluded from decision-making to shape policy. Yet councils also risk being viewed, like career politicians, as being out of touch with the concerns of ordinary people, which would raise similar issues of political legitimacy. Engaging with the wider public at regular intervals through outreach events, presentations, and discussions at citizens' cafés could allay such concerns. The development of a culture of participation within a future council and, progressively, within a community or across a region is an exercise in patience. Citizens and politicians alike need support and advice throughout this transition, as the work over the last decade of the Office for Future-Related Issues in Vorarlberg, Austria, has shown. It takes time to create innovative communities that involve citizens in planning and decision-making processes and acknowledge their responsibility toward future generations. But communities such as those emerging with the support of the "Future Communities"[130] rural development programme in Austria make ideal sites for the establishment of future councils.

In terms of the scheduling of and choice of venues for future councils' activities, we don't wish to make any specific recommendations about how frequently future councils should meet. Those with some experience of group processes will understand how important it is to establish a regular schedule that participants can organize their lives around. Like any organization, future councils will need to establish their own rhythms to avoid overtaxing participants or fostering an excessively casual attitude.

Location matters, even in public participation. The buildings in which future councils convene should be places where citizens feel welcome. They should be characterized by an inviting architectural and visual design that provides a good working environment. The challenge of finding suitable facilities for both the ongoing operations of the councils and for their outreach activities touches on the need to both restore sites of civic culture that have fallen into neglect and to create new spaces for the political public sphere. A neglect of and even disdain for public spaces that are neither commercial nor related to work or leisure is a conspicuous aspect of postmodern cities, which reflect a culture focused on commerce, events, and entertainment. According to political scientist John Parkinson, spaces can be public in four ways—that is, in terms of accessibility, use of public resources, common impacts, or as a stage for the performance of public roles.[131] Identifying sites that fulfill these requirements will no doubt be challenging.

Because future councils will only hold public sessions occasionally (citizens' café events, for example), they will need to use other means to make their deliberations, findings, and plans public. The creation of an online platform to provide transparency and facilitate dialog would be one way to achieve this. Future councils could also "go walkabout" from time to time and engage with religious communities, charitable associations, schools, companies, and the like. Outreach events such as this would serve to maintain a political public sphere that is otherwise increasingly constrained.

Results

We anticipate that future councils will produce well-founded and broadly comprehensible public-policy recommendations, complemented by other outputs such as public events and Web-based communication. These recommendations will be disseminated to the relevant legislative bodies and administrations, other people involved in decision-making processes (whether formally or informally), and the public.

At least three issues must be addressed in this context. First, how will dissenting opinions be documented? The fact that future councils will not always arrive at a unanimous position is not, in our view, problematic. Indeed, it may well be beneficial to identify and explore dissenting views by developing alternative future scenarios. This is preferable to the mere parroting of platitudes (e.g. "Our city should be more attractive") and non-binding objectives (e.g. aspirations to reduce emissions by 90 percent by 2020) and would increase the transparency of future councils.

The second and more significant question is, what can be done to ensure that council recommendations are carefully considered within the other branches of government and—when they are rejected—that decision-makers provide an adequate and detailed response? Because future councils will address issues that are frequently neglected in everyday parliamentary and administrative practice, representative democratic institutions should be required to respond to future councils within a reasonable period. The implementation of mandatory feedback mechanisms to connect local councils, state legislatures, and parliaments with future councils will be crucial to the success of this model of public participation. These mechanisms must make clear whether and how decision-making institutions have addressed issues raised by future councils. The adoption of such mechanisms would impose a duty on decision-making bodies to justify their actions (or lack thereof) to future councils, municipalities, and entire regions, not only in the present moment but also in the months and years following. The relevant rules of procedure must include this duty to encourage future councils, the public, and political leaders to engage in meaningful dialog on equal terms. The obligation placed on future councils to report on their activities at regular intervals is paralleled by the requirement that the executive and legislative branches consider and respond within a reasonable period. Where the findings and recommendations of a future council are likely to have a significant impact on the political process, decision-makers could ask the electorate to voice its opinion in a referendum.

The third question is, what can be done to minimize rivalry between future councils, city mayors, and other elected representatives? Ideally, the play of democratic institutions will give rise to mutual appreciation, but it is likely that future councils will occasionally be drawn into power plays. This can be prevented by encouraging future councils to develop a sense of collective awareness, grounded in the personalities of their members. As a rule, future councils risk irrelevance if they are either too radical or too mainstream in their findings. Social innovations tend to arise on the periphery within a culture that values doubt and dissent.

Finances

While public participation is frequently mentioned in discussions of the reform of policymaking, decision-makers have traditionally been reluctant to provide the funding necessary to ensure its success. The establishment and operation of future councils and their ancillary organs will undeniably require administrative and political institutions at all levels to make substantial investments. Municipal, regional, and national institutions could mobilize the necessary financial resources. Alternatively, an endowment fund dedicated to this purpose could be established. Sociologist Ortwin Renn favours the establishment of a state-owned foundation furnished with the financial resources necessary to organize participation processes. Crowdfunding could provide an alternative source of funding. These options would safeguard the independence of public participation and reduce the likelihood that conflicts of interest with local governments would arise. In our view, the proposed model of participation would be best served by the creation of a national foundation whose local offices would provide support for future councils and facilitate communication between councils, administrative bodies, and citizens.[132] The pros and cons of both funding models—direct government versus foundation—need further study.

In addition to the salaries payable to administrative workers, future councils will require enough funding to compensate council members, who will need to take leaves of absence from their regular employment to participate in council deliberations. (Lay judges in the German judicial system receive around six euros per hour under a similar scheme.) To foster inclusion, council members should also have access to various support services, such as professional childcare and transportation for individuals with disabilities. Future councils cannot operate as community services staffed by volunteers, nor will it be possible to fully compensate council members for their loss of earnings. Instead, members will occupy a hybrid semi-professional role in what is a voluntary public office. Participants will, of course, respond to monetary incentives differently, and this can have a troubling impact on the functioning of a future council. In general, however, we believe that it is important to acknowledge the work performed by council members in this way.

Conclusion

This chapter has offered an overview of how future councils might operate. As permanent institutions embedded within communities, municipalities, countries, and supranational organizations, future councils will be tasked with identifying key future challenges and proposing possible solutions, and the legislative and executive branches of governments will respond to their recommendations in a timely and substantive manner. Depending on the political level at which they are situated, each council will consist of between fifteen and fifty randomly selected representatives, reflecting the diversity of the population and especially its generational profile. Members will meet regularly and receive a modest allowance to cover their expenses. Future council members will serve for a period of two years and will be supported by administrative teams with experience in both facilitation and general management.

We hope that future councils will counterbalance the structural deficiencies of deliberative democracy in its current form by integrating the emotional dimension of political debate. The establishment of future councils as permanent bodies will, we believe, enable them to overcome the often-inconstant nature of participatory practices and better reflect the diversity of views within local, regional, and national populations than experts can. By bringing together citizens of different generations, future councils will highlight the potential of political practices that look beyond contemporary horizons and seek to address future challenges within current policy debates and decision-making.

The ideas presented here have been trialed in several pilot projects,[133] enabling us to assess their feasibility. In addition to this, we have outlined them to members of the public and a range of experts, who have raised several concerns that we wish to address here relating to the selection process and the length of the mandate. Critics suggested that less formal opportunities for participation—responsive, one-off councils, for example—might be more attractive to citizens. Considering the trend toward more informal and temporary forms of engagement, they ask, would it not be better to adopt a more flexible, low-threshold format that would enable larger numbers of citizens to participate? Some have also argued that the targeted recruitment of specific groups could undermine the entire process, leaving future councils mired in challenges to their political legitimacy. It is our belief however that ensuring the involvement of the relevant social groups merely requires the creation of an enabling environment through, for example, the provision of childcare services. Meanwhile, others have suggested that our focus on real-time, face-to-face communication ignores the vast possibilities of Web-based political communication.

Others expressed doubts as to whether an experimental body of this kind, tasked with addressing challenges at the local level, albeit from a global perspective, can resolve the crisis of democratic legitimacy outlined in the opening chapter. Would future councils not be subject to the same widespread disaffection with political institutions? The public, they argue, might well place as little trust in future councils as they currently do in governments and parliaments. What is the appeal, they ask, of future councils to disaffected citizens and those members of the public who prefer to engage with selected issues on an ad hoc basis? Some others have also questioned whether the creation of future councils would heighten the potential for conflict and confusion in political decision-making by introducing a "rival player." Would it not be more effective, they ask, to develop a format that brings representatives from civil society and administrative bodies together with career politicians from the very outset, or one that draws on the expertise of established change-makers within a specific sector (for example, sustainability or refugee policy)?

All these objections and concerns have some merit. Future councils alone will not solve the legitimacy deficits of contemporary democratic politics. But the broad development of a consultative branch could, in our view, improve both the quality and sustainability of politics and ensure that citizens can assert their concerns within the political process. Our concept is not revolutionary. Rather, it is pragmatic, experimental, and ameliorative; that is, it aims to bring about gradual improvement. The success (or failure) of this experiment will depend on the level of commitment made to it, its proper implementation, and the willingness of political actors to engage meaningfully with the findings of future councils. If these conditions are met, future councils will indeed advance democracy. The notion that our proposal might prompt the development of a range of divergent or rival models of future-oriented policymaking is a welcome one. But whatever model is adopted, it is important to remember that inadequate institutionalization measures, coupled with a fixation on short-term outcomes (by governments and citizens alike), have in the past caused public participation processes to under-perform, resulting in disappointing outcomes.

Chapter Five

FUTURE COUNCILS: A PATHWAY TO TRANSNATIONAL DEMOCRACY?

Traditional federalism often cuts across complex policy areas, particularly in relation to issues of future importance. Decision-making at each level is imperfect. As a rule, for example, the more locally a decision is made, the more likely it is to be influenced by NIMBYism, or the Florian Principle; conversely, the further removed a decision is from those affected, the less likely decision-makers are to grasp its complexity. With this in mind, we propose the creation of a multilevel network of future councils that operates "from the bottom up"—that is, from the local and municipal levels, through the regional and state levels, to the national and European levels—and whose output feeds into parliamentary and direct democratic decision-making. At the supranational level of the European Union, we call for the creation of a permanent European Future Council. Its tasks would be to put important future topics on the agenda and to advise the European Parliament, Council, and Commission. By giving European citizens a more direct voice in decision-making, the council could also help to counteract both the growing unease over the lack of transparency in Brussels (the EU's unofficial capital) and rising anti-EU populism. Mutual solidarity and loyalty to the EU's political institutions can only develop when the integrative power that comes from democratic participation is given space to flourish at the transnational level. Crucially, the findings of a European Future Council must actually feed into European decision-making processes in order for citizens to recognize the council's value and legitimacy.

Participation Across Borders

At the supranational level, the European Commission and the European Parliament have already tested several projects, processes, and methods for transnational and multilingual public participation. Following the disastrous rejection of the EU Constitution in referendums in France and the Netherlands in 2005 and with support for the EU dwindling among European populations, the EU developed a communications strategy called Plan D (for democracy, dialog, and discussion) and launched the e-Europe Initiative. As a result, the EU conducted twenty-three transnational participation processes between 2005 and 2010, with an estimated one hundred thousand citizens participating.

The most comprehensive and complex of these processes was the European Citizens' Consultations project. Its stated aims were, first, to narrow the gap between the EU and its citizens and, second, to explore long-term participation as a political instrument at the European level. Over fifteen hundred citizens from twenty-seven member states, all randomly selected based on socio-demographic criteria, took part in each process and deliberated on the future of Europe.[134] As with many similar events in Europe, the project was organized by a civil society organization—in this case, the Belgian King Baudouin Foundation. Participants expressed great satisfaction at having been invited to debate Europe's future in one- or two-day sessions and reported that they subsequently felt better informed, had a more positive attitude to the European project, and in some cases changed their views during the discussions. However, many expressed disappointment that politicians and officials failed to take enough account of the results of these "democratic experiments."[135]

In the end, such selective and temporary processes had only a minor impact on the formation of public opinion and decision-making processes in the EU. Their impact would certainly have been greater if mechanisms had been established to link a more sophisticated version of the citizens' dialog with the EU's formal decision-making processes; instead, the project was broken off without explanation. In 2011 the EU created the European Citizens' Initiative to give EU citizens a say in decision-making.[136] Under the initiative, citizens can compel the EU Commission to consider specific legislative proposals by submitting a petition with at least a million signatories drawn from at least seven member states. Yet this instrument of direct democracy primarily serves organized interest groups that have the financial or technological means to collect the requisite signatures within the twelve-month deadline. It certainly does not offer a suitable framework for discussion of future challenges that can transcend borders and build European civic and political consciousness. If the European Union wants to make a direct connection with its citizens, the only way to do so is to begin a discussion with them. The democratic legitimacy of the European Union—and perhaps its continued existence—depends on successfully involving its citizens.

French President Emmanuel Macron recently opened the door to a broad debate on the future of European participation. In a speech delivered at Paris's Sorbonne University in September 2017, Macron put forward the idea of engaging the citizens of Europe in what he referred to as "democratic conventions" to afford them a voice beyond the scope of elections. These public consultations would focus debate in member states in the run-up to European parliamentary elections. Macron's idea suggests moving away from a model of European integration as an elite project toward a citizen-led model in which open-ended discussions rather than yes/no referendums determine outcomes. German Chancellor Angela Merkel took up this idea and hosted a series of so-called citizen dialogs on the future of Europe in May 2018. These events have been criticized, however, as poorly organized and unrepresentative. To provide a credible opportunity for dialog, events should have been held in cities and towns throughout Germany and France, with a randomly selected sample of citizens in each location. These events also lacked any clear method of feeding into national and European decision-making processes. Moreover, it is highly unlikely that such consultations could be staged in all the other member states. These citizen dialogs at the national level fell short of the benchmark set by the transnational model of participation implemented by the European Commission between 2005 and 2010.

Laboratories of European Democracy

We therefore propose not only a revival of the earlier transnational participation initiatives but also the creation of a permanent European Future Council. While the main job of the European Future Council would be advising the EU's governing institutions on future policy issues, it could also initiate individual participation processes to address pressing issues such as the development of a common response to immigration to the Schengen Area (the area comprising the EU member states that have abolished passport and other border controls along their mutual borders). By collating and communicating the results of individual dialog-based participation processes, the European Future Council could act as an advocate for European citizens. (The EU might also establish future councils at the regional level—for example, one for countries bordering the Mediterranean or those in tri-border regions—to discuss questions of medium- or long-term regional policy.)

Among the key issues that the European Future Council would be well suited to address is the common European energy policy—a central issue for the future of Europe. Energy consumption accounts, directly or indirectly, for 80 percent of all greenhouse gas emissions, and the European Council has pledged to reduce carbon dioxide emissions by 80 to 95 percent compared to 1990 levels by the year 2050.[137] Yet, the success of efforts to decarbonize our energy system and enter an age of renewable energy will depend on whether we manage to develop a sustainable common energy policy and expand transnational grid infrastructures.

In contrast to the usual participatory processes set up to examine specific infrastructure projects, a European Future Council could focus on broad scenarios at the supranational level. Additionally, it could identify potential conflicts of interest and values at an early stage. And it could develop specific proposals for dealing fairly with the social burdens of the energy transition and for building the kind of European commonwealth its citizens would like. With the future of Europe depending more than ever on the Franco-German axis, the two governments could initially establish a binational future council to advance the European Energy Union, for example, or the implementation of ambitious decarbonization goals. This much is certain: the transformation of the European energy system will have far-reaching consequences for how we live in the future. Delivering on the promise of a European energy transition will require broad democratic legitimation and the active involvement of Europe's citizens.

Increasing participation in EU decision-making on essential issues, like the energy transition, would increase transparency in Brussels and combat growing anti-EU populism but only if participating citizens see that EU decision-makers take seriously the results of the council's work. The European Future Council would ideally be part of a larger network of future councils in all member states. In this sense, it could be initiated "from the top"—from the European Commission and/or European Parliament, for example—or it could evolve "from below"—from local, regional, and national future councils, with each delegating a number of members to the next level above.

In fact, the network of future councils we envision would enable those who wish to participate to move back and forth between the local, national, and European levels. A person in Germany, for example, might first join a community-level future council, later move to the federal level, and eventually become a German representative in the European Future Council. (Participants might also move the other way, being first appointed to the European or a national future council before subsequently working for a local one.) Even if future councils were to recruit members entirely separately at each level—meaning there would be no flow of members between levels—we are confident that greater political participation across the board would emerge from this. Local councils could initiate debates and campaigns or focus on specific topics, leading to a trickle-up effect that would reinforce the work of future councils at all levels. In the same way, an initiative from a council in Brussels, Warsaw, or Berlin could make its way from top to bottom through a trickle-down process. In this sense, "top" and "bottom" do not have to be fixed points in a political hierarchy but can constantly interact and resolve mutual conflicts as part of a democratic process.

The different languages and political cultures of EU member states mean that a European future council will be more complex than that of a single community or country. One issue that must be considered is whether English can work as the common language for all participants or whether future councils will need to use interpreters, as is usual in EU institutions. The distances that delegates will need to travel are longer and the logistics more complicated than in future councils at other levels. European Future Council meetings would not always have to be held in Brussels; members could convene in different European cities. Considering this organizational and logistical complexity, it would make sense to schedule sessions only every two or three months, but then for two days at a time. The European Future Council would present and discuss its conclusions and interim findings at public events. Like local future councils, it would have no imperative mandate, but the three decision-making institutions in the EU—Parliament, Commission, and Council—would be obliged to formally respond to its recommendations (and questions) within a timeframe considered reasonable for the issues under discussion.

Such a permanent European consultative body—as a "fourth authority"—would provide an important boost for Europe as a political entity, support the evolution of a European culture of participation and citizenship, and finally breathe life into the basic principles of European democracy.[138]

Epilogue
THE FOURTH BRANCH
OF GOVERNMENT

Situated between Munich and Miesbach, the German town of Weyarn (population 3,400) has been described in newspaper reports as the scene of a veritable "democratic miracle." The transformation began with a regional village renewal scheme that included participatory elements, which in Weyarn took the form of citizens' workshops and working groups. These groups addressed challenges such as intergenerational cooperation and the goal of transitioning the township to renewable energy by 2025. Proposals developed in these workshops were (and still are) sent to the local council and administration, which took them seriously. Over the years, this ongoing experiment has forged a functional relationship between the legislative and consultative bodies. Although individual members of the local were initially fearful of "surrendering power," over time they have come to see this model of participation—now formally acknowledged in the township's statutes as the "two-pillar model"—as an "enrichment" that has strengthened the legislature. According to officials, this "second chamber" has succeeded in bridging the gap between decision-makers and citizens and has not been hijacked by "party politics or personal interests."[139]

Over the course of the four decades between the antinuclear protests at Wyhl that were hailed by *Der Spiegel* as heralding the creation of a "fourth estate" (and with which we began this book) and the "democratic miracle" of Weyarn, the consultative has evolved and emerged as the fourth branch of government.[140] Within this slender volume we have outlined our proposal to continue this development by establishing future councils as the institutional cornerstone of the consultative branch. Our proposal embodies principles of intergenerational justice and a vision of humanity and society based on cooperation and conviviality. The creation of future councils would expand democracy as we know and value it and address the multiple challenges currently facing democratic countries.

Meaningful participation offers an alternative to the paranoid and angry populism that has recently spread like wildfire throughout the world and taken shape in movements like the Tea Party in the United States, PEGIDA (Patriotic Europeans Against the Islamization of the West) in Germany, and the Front National in France. But for this experiment in democracy to succeed, it must be conducted at just the right temperature. Technocratic approaches, with their focus on practical constraints, have a chilling effect on political engagement. Conversely, populism causes democratic societies to overheat, as aggressive resentments fuel social tensions. Indignation, the willingness to protest, and even anger are respectable passions and drivers of political action, but they need to be channeled into constructive forums without diminishing their emotional power.

Politics, or what German statesperson Otto von Bismarck called "the art of the possible," has always acted as a barrier to visionary change. But only by pushing at that barrier can we develop a feeling that our world can change for the better. Addressing significant issues that will have long-term effects on future generations will require political spaces that offer sufficient scope for diverse worldviews, constructive controversy, genuine dialog, and mindful responsibility. As a principle of governance participation is tied to a model of citizenship that is inclusive of ethnic, religious, cultural, and gender diversity and excludes discrimination. The democratic principle of "one person, one vote" applies irrespective of social inequalities and differences, and it is on this basis that citizens must be empowered to take political action. If people lack the means of participation, they tend to become apathetic or angry. Conversely, when opportunities for participation exist, people naturally get involved in public life. Participation in the consultative, in the future councils proposed here, will require neither a constant nor a lifelong commitment. Yet the ability of individuals to engage in such participatory processes will depend on many factors and vary over time.

The success of future councils will depend not only on the willingness of citizens to engage in participation but also on the willingness of decision-makers to take seriously the collective wisdom of ordinary citizens that future councils embody. For this reason, we address this book not only to citizens but also to those forward-thinking professionals in public administration and politics who must weather the vagaries of public participation. We hope this book will empower them to place public participation on a more stable foundation and enable them to see the consultative branch not as an unwelcome rival but as a vital element in the strengthening of a divided democracy. Our proposal is informed by a wealth of experience gathered in various debates and participation processes, and yet it will no doubt continue to evolve and improve as it is put into practice.

ACKNOWLEDGMENTS

The foundations for this book were laid in the intellectually stimulating atmosphere of the "Culture of Participation" research area at the Institute for Advanced Study in the Humanities, or KWI, in Essen. The text is informed by the rich insights from the field of public participation provided by researchers Mathis Danelzik, Giulia Molinengo, and Lea Schmitt. Teresa Bartolomei Vasconcelos, Frederic Hanusch, Jan-Hendrik Kamlage, Henrike Knappe, Anne Kroh, Louise Röska-Hardy, and Charles Taylor all provided valuable input at various stages of this project. We also wish to thank Manfred Hellrigl, Christoph Möllers, Philippe Narval, Daniel Oppold, and Ina Richter for their detailed appraisals and constructive criticism. The legal scholar and former judge of the Federal Constitutional Court of Germany, Brun-Otto Bryde; former President of the Bundestag, Norbert Lammert; and former federal minister and founding director of the Institute for Advanced Sustainability Studies (IASS), Klaus Töpfer, all shared their thoughts on early drafts of this text and offered insights from the perspectives of each of the three branches of the German government. We also wish to thank our colleagues Petra Dobner, Hans J. Lietzmann, and Ortwin Renn for their contributions. Our thanks also go to Nora Schecke for her assistance with the literature review.

For their editorial guidance and support, we offer our sincere gratitude to the publisher of our English edition, Between the Lines, and Amanda Crocker in particular. We are especially grateful to Graham Smith for his generous and insightful critique of the English text. And last but not least, we thank Damian Harrison and Stephen Roche for their work on the translation of this book, Ludwig Wegner and Christoph Becker for their invaluable support, and Joseph Tohill for his superb editorial work. All responsibility for any remaining errors or idiosyncrasies lies with the authors alone.

NOTES

1   Max Kaase, "The Challenge of the 'Participatory Revolution' in Pluralist Democracies," *International Political Science Review* 5 (1984): 299–318.

2   The route will now end in Landshut rather than Grundremmingen and will make extensive use of underground cables. http://www.br.de/nachrichten/oberpfalz/inhalt/ostbayernring-tennet-raumordnungsverfahren-100.html (site discontinued).

3   "Bürgerproteste—die vierte Gewalt," *Der Spiegel,* March 21, 1977, http://www.spiegel.de/spiegel/print/d-40941743.html.

4   Thomas Leif and Rudolf Speth, eds., *Die fünfte Gewalt: Lobbyismus in Deutschland* (Wiesbaden: Springer, 2006).

5   Christoph Möllers, *Die drei Gewalten: Legitimation der Gewaltengliederung in Verfassungsstaat: Europäischer Integration und Internationalisierung* (Weilerswist: Velbrück Wissenschaft Verlag, 2008).

6   Basic Law for the Federal Republic of Germany (GG), Article 20 (2), Berlin 2015, https://www.gesetze-im-internet.de/englisch_gg/englisch_gg.html.

7   "Lammert droht mit Ablehnung von TTIP," *Zeit Online,*
     October 28, 2015, http://www.zeit.de/.

8   Franz Walter noted this in connection with the Eurozone
     crisis and the associated bailouts in "EFSF-Votum im
     Bundestag: Land ohne Opposition," *Der Spiegel,* October
     26, 2011, http://www.spiegel.de/. See also Philip Norton,
     Does Parliament Matter? (New York: Harvester Wheat-
     sheaf, 1993).

9   Wilhelm Hennis, *Politikwissenschaft und politisches Den-
     ken. Politikwissenschaftliche Abhandlungen II* (Tübingen:
     Mohr Siebeck, 2000).

10   See Mark B. Brown et al., *Politikberatung und Parlament*
     (Opladen: Verlag Barbara Budrich, 2006); Birger Priddat,
     ed., *Politikberatung: Prozesse, Logik und Ökonomie* (Mar-
     burg: Metropolis, 2009). Among the temporary bodies
     convened by the German executive branch is the Com-
     mission on the Storage of High-Level Radioactive Waste
     (the Repository Commission), which brings together
     thirty-three representatives from the scientific communi-
     ty, civil society, and members of state governments and
     the German parliament.

11   James Surowiecki, *The Wisdom of Crowds: Why the Many
     are Smarter than the Few and How Collective Wisdom
     Shapes Business, Economies, Societies, and Nations* (New
     York: Doubleday, 2004). See also Daniel Innerarity, *The
     Democracy of Knowledge* (New York: Bloomsbury, 2013).

12   Robert Inglehart, *The Silent Revolution: Changing Values
     and Political Styles among Western Publics* (Princeton, NJ:
     Princeton University Press, 1977); Kaase, "The Challenge
     of the 'Participatory Revolution'"; Pippa Norris,

Democratic Phoenix: Reinventing Political Activism (Cambridge, UK: Cambridge University Press, 2008).

13 Max Kaase, "Partizipation," in *Wörterbuch Staat und Politik*, ed. Dieter Nohlen (Bonn: Piper, 1995), 521–527.

14 See, for example, http://www.joachimsikora.de/index. php/site-administrator/11-debattenbeitrag-2.

15 Hans J. Lietzmann, Alexandra Ehlers, and Bettina Ülpenich, *Bürgerbeteiligung in den Kommunen: Die 'neue Gewaltenteilung' in der lokalen Politik,* Gutachten der Forschungsstelle Bürgerbeteiligung im Auftrag der GAR NRW (Düsseldorf: GAR NRW, 2013).

16 Seventy-six percent of German citizens have expressed a desire for greater public involvement in decision-making, and 73 percent of the population has expressed their willingness to participate in citizen forums. (Incidentally, a majority of those surveyed held negative views of web-based forms of participation.) See *Partizipation im Wandel: Unsere Demokratie zwischen Wählen, Mitmachen und Entscheiden*, ed. Bertelsmann Stiftung and Staatsministerium Baden-Württemberg (Gütersloh: Verlag Bertelsmann Stiftung, 2014).

17 A. Giddens, *Modernity and Self-Identity* (Cambridge: Polity Press, 1991); Claus Leggewie and Harald Welzer, *Das Ende der Welt, wie wir sie kannten: Klima, Zukunft und die Chancen der Demokratie* (Frankfurt: S. Fischer 2009).

18 This line of critique views democracy as a "Western idea" (which it was) that has been created by acts of colonial violence and social exploitation. See, for example, Giorgio Agamben et al, *Democracy in What State?* (New York: Columbia University Press, 2011); and Alain Badiou,

Pornographie du temps présent (Paris: Librairie Arthème Fayard, 2013). For a critical perspective, see Klaus von Beyme, *From Post-Democracy to Neo-Democracy* (Cham, Switzerland: Springer, 2018); and Simon Tormey, *The End of Representative Politics* (Cambridge: Polity Press, 2015).

19 See the empirical work of Pippa Norris, *Democratic Phoenix: Agencies, Repertoires & Targets of Political Activism* (Cambridge, MA: APSA, 2002). Freedom House maps are available online at https://freedomhouse.org/report/freedom-world-2015/maps. For a sophisticated approach to measuring the quality of democracies, see Marc Bühlmann et al., *The Quality of Democracy: Democracy Barometer for Established Democracies* (Zürich: National Centre of Competence in Research Democracy of the Swiss National Science Foundation, 2008).

20 Freedom House, *Freedom in the World 2018* (Washington, 2018), https://freedomhouse.org/.

21 Colin Crouch, *Post-Democracy* (Oxford: Polity, 2004); and Ingolfur Blühdorn, *Simulative Demokratie: Neue Politik nach der postdemokratischen Wende* (Frankfurt: Suhrkamp, 2013). For a contrary view, see Dirk Jörke, "Bürgerbeteiligung in der Postdemokratie," *Aus Politik und Zeitgeschichte* 1–2 (2011): 13–18; and Dirk Jörke, "Was kommt nach der Postdemokratie?," *Vorgänge: Zeitschrift für Bürgerrechte und Gesellschaftspolitik* 190 (2010): 17–25.

22 See Armin Schäfer, *Der Verlust politischer Gleichheit: Warum die sinkende Wahlbeteiligung der Demokratie schadet* (Frankfurt: Campus Verlag, 2015); and Armin

Schäfer and Harald Schoen, "Mehr Demokratie, aber nur für wenige? Der Zielkonflikt zwischen mehr Beteiligung und politischer Gleichheit," *Leviathan* 41, no. 1 (2013): 94–120.

23 See *Partizipation im Wandel*.

24 Institut für Demoskopie Allensbach/Bertelsmann Stiftung, *Einstellungen zur sozialen Marktwirtschaft* in *Deutschland am Jahresanfang 2010: Erkenntnisse ausrepräsentativen Trendfortschreibungen*, November 2010, https://www.ifd-allensbach.de/uploads/tx_studies/7472_ Soziale_Marktwirtschaft.pdf.

25 Karl Polanyi, *The Great Transformation: The Political and Economic Origins of Our Time* (Boston: Beacon Press, 2001).

26 See David Runciman, *How Democracy Ends* (New York: Basic Books, 2018).

27 Richard Hofstadter, *The Paranoid Style in American Politics* (New York: Alfred A. Knopf, 1965).

28 Max Scheler, *Ressentiment* (Milwaukee, WI: Marquette University Press, 2010).

29 Ironically, Viktor Orbán entered politics in the late 1980s as the rising star of Fidesz—Hungarian Civic Alliance, a new party he co-founded. Fidesz restricted membership to persons aged thirty-five or under in an attempt to distance itself from the *ancien régime*, post-socialist corruption and the disrepute of right-wing politics in the late twentieth century. By way of example, see "Full text of Viktor Orbán's speech at Băile Tuşnad (Tusnádfürdő) of 26 July 2014," *Budapest Beacon*, July 29, 2014, https:// budapestbeacon.com/.

30   This section focuses on right-wing populism; for a discussion of left-wing populism, see Chantal Mouffe, *For a Left Populism* (London: Verso, 2018).

31   Ivan Krastev, "The Populist Moment," *Eurozine*, September 18, 2007, https://www.eurozine.com/.

32   The debate over animal rights offers some useful analogies. Some authors, for example, refer to animals as a third "constituency," or the other species. See, for example, Andrew Dobson, "Democracy and Nature: Speaking and Listening," *Political Studies* 58 (2010): 752–768; Andrew Dobson, *Justice and the Environment: Conceptions of Environmental Sustainability and Theories of Distributive Justice* (Oxford: Oxford University Press, 1998); and Bruno Latour, *The Politics of Nature: How to Bring the Sciences into Democracy* (Cambridge, MA: Harvard University Press, 2004).

33   United Nations World Commission on Environment and Development, *Report of the World Commission on Environment and Development: Our Common Future* (1987), http://www.un-documents.net/our-common-future.pdf

34   Schwesig outlined her proposal on several occasions in connection with the twenty-fifth anniversary of the UN Convention on the Rights of the Child. See, for example, the German daily newspaper *Die Welt*, November 21, 2014.

35   Achim Goerres and Guido Tiemann, "Kinder an die Macht? Die politischen Konsequenzen des stellvertretenden Elternwahlrechts," *Politische Vierteljahresschrift* 50 (2009): 50–74.

36 This stands in the tradition of the American pragmatist John Dewey. See, for example, Charles F. Sabel, "Dewey, Democracy, and Democratic Experimentalism," *Contemporary Pragmatism* 9, no. 2 (December 2012): 35-55. For more on institutionalizing the interests of future generations, see Andrew Dobson, "Representative Democracy and the Environment," in *Democracy and the Environment: Problems and Principles*, ed. William M. Lafferty and James Meadowcroft (Cheltenham: Edward Elgar Publishing, 1996), 124–139; Kristian Skagen Ekeli, "Electoral Design, Submajority Rules and Representation of Future Generations," in *Institutions for Future Generations*, ed. Axel Gosseries and Iñigo González Ricoy (Oxford: Oxford University Press, 2015); Kristian Skagen Ekeli, "Giving a Voice to Posterity: Deliberative Democracy and Representation of Future People," *Journal of Agricultural and Environmental Ethics* 18 (2005): 429–450; Dennis F. Thompson, "Representing Future Generations: Political Presentism and Democratic Trusteeship," *Critical Review of International Social and Political Philosophy* 13 (2010): 17–37.

37 Jürgen Habermas, *Between Facts and Norms: Contributions to a Discourse Theory of Law and Democracy* (Cambridge, MA: MIT Press, 1996), 287ff.

38 See James S. Fishkin, *Democracy and Deliberation: New Directions for Democratic Reform* (New Haven, CT: Yale University Press, 1991); James S. Fishkin and Robert C. Luskin, "Experimenting with a Democratic Ideal: Deliberative Polling and Public Opinion," *Acta Politica* 40 (2005): 284–298.

39   Carolyn J. Lukensmeyer and Steve Brigham, "Taking Democracy to Scale: Creating a Town Hall Meeting for the Twenty-First Century," *National Civic Review* 91 (2002): 351–366.

40   See the wiki-platform participedia.net, which catalogs and compares democratic innovations from around the world.

41   Pierre Rosanvallon, *Counter-Democracy: Politics in the Age of Distrust* (Cambridge: Cambridge University Press, 2008). For critical views on "deliberative surrogate-democracy," see Danny Michelsen and Franz Walter, *Unpolitische Demokratie: Zur Krise der Repräsentation* (Berlin: Suhrkamp, 2013), chapter 3; and Wolfgang Merkel, *Nur schöner Schein? Demokratische Innovationen in Theorie und Praxis* (Frankfurt: Otto Brenner Stiftung, 2015), 42ff.

42   Dirk Jörke, "Die Versprechen der Demokratie und die Grenzen der Deliberation," *Zeitschrift für Politikwissenschaft* 20 (2010): 269–290. For a contrary view, see Michael Walzer, "Deliberation, and what else?," in *Deliberative Politics: Essays on Democracy and Disagreement*, ed. Stephen Macedo (New York/Oxford: Oxford University Press, 1999), 58–69.

43   Michael E. Morrell, *Empathy and Democracy: Feeling, Thinking, and Deliberation* (University Park, PA: Penn State University Press, 2010); Charles Taylor, *Wieviel Gemeinschaft braucht die Demokratie? Aufsätze zur praktischen Philosophie* (Frankfurt: Suhrkamp, 2001).

44   John Stuart Mill, *On Liberty* (London, 1913), 7.

45   Jorge Adriano Lubenow "Public Sphere and Deliberative Democracy in Jürgen Habermas: Theoretical Model and

Critical Discourses," *American Journal of Sociological Research* 2, no. 4 (2012): 58-71.

46 Hannah Arendt, *Was ist Politik? Fragmente aus dem Nachlass* (Munich: Piper, 1993), 97.

47 Brigitte Geißel, *Kritische Bürger: Gefahr oder Ressource für die Demokratie?* (Frankfurt: Campus Verlag, 2011).

48 Harald Heinrichs, Katina Kuhn, and Jens Newig, eds., *Nachhaltige Gesellschaft: Welche Rolle für Partizipation und Kooperation?* (Wiesbaden: VS Verlag, Springer, 2011).

49 Helmut Klages, *Wertorientierungen im Wandel: Rückblick, Gegenwartsanalyse, Prognosen* (Frankfurt and New York: Campus Verlag, 1984); Paul Nolte, *Was ist Demokratie? Geschichte und Gegenwart* (Munich: C. H. Beck, 2012), 348–355

50 Ulrich von Alemann, ed., *Partizipation, Demokratisierung, Mitbestimmung: Problemstellung und Literatur in Politik, Wirtschaft, Bildung und Wissenschaft; Eine Einführung* (Opladen: Springer, 1975); and Carole Pateman, *Participation and Democratic Theory* (Cambridge: Cambridge University Press, 1970).

51 Brian Wampler, Stephanie McNulty, and Michael Touchton, *Participatory Budgeting: Spreading Across the Globe,* January 2018, Transparency and Accountability Initiative, http://transparency-initiative.org/.

52 Carsten Herzberg, Anja Röcke, and Yves Sintomer, "Von Porto Alegre nach Europa: Möglichkeiten und Grenzen des Bürgerhaushalts," in *Kommunaler Bürgerhaushalt in Theorie und Praxis am Beispiel Potsdams*, ed. Jochen Franzke and Heinz Kleger (Potsdam: Universitätsverlag Potsdam, 2006), 188–205; and Gianpaolo Baiocchi, *Militants and*

Citizens: The Politics of Participatory Democracy in Porto Alegre (Stanford, CA: Stanford University Press, 2005).

53   Archon Fung and Erik O. Wright, *Deepening Democracy: Institutional Innovations in Empowered Participatory Governance* (London: Verso, 2003).

54   Yves Sintomer, *Le pouvoir au peuple: Jurys citoyens, tirage au sort et démocratie participative* (Paris: Editions La Découverte, 2007); Loïc Blondiaux, *Le nouvel esprit de la démocratie: Actualité de la démocratie participative* (Paris: Le Seuil, 2008).

55   Roland Roth, *Bürgermacht: Eine Streitschrift für mehr Partizipation* (Hamburg: Edition Körber Stiftung, 2011); Norbert Kersting, "Das Zeitalter der politischen Beteiligung: Partizipativer Wandel oder politisches Disengagement," in *Zeitalter der Partizipation*, ed. Lothar Harles and Dirk Lange (Schwalbach: Wochenschau Verlag, 2015), 49–62; Oscar W. Gabriel and Norbert Kersting, "Partizipation auf kommunaler Ebene: Politisches Engagement in deutschen Kommunen: Strukturen und Wirkungen auf die politischen Einstellungen von Bürgerschaft, Politik und Verwaltung," in *Partizipation im Wandel*, 43–184; and Brigitte Geißel and Norbert Kersting, "Zwischen Parteiendemokratie und partizipativen Innovationen: Beteiligungskultur in Deutschland," *eNewsletter Wegweiser Bürgergesellschaft* 12 (June 6, 2014).

56   Ortwin Renn, Thomas Webler, and Peter Wiedemann, eds., *Fairness and Competence in Citizen Participation: Evaluating Models for Environmental Discourse* (Dordrecht: Springer, 1995).

57 The Association of German Cities (*Deutscher Städtetag*) is an umbrella organization that represents the interests of larger German cities in relation to the German government, federal states, the European Union, and non-state entities. "Deutscher Städtetag: Bürgerbeteiligung als Chance begreifen—lebendige lokale Demokratie fördern," *Pressemitteilung*, November 22, 2013, http://www.staedtetag.de/dst/inter/presse/mitteilungen/067896/index.html.

58 "Aarhus Convention," Participation and Sustainable Development in Europe (website), Austrian Ministry of the Environment, http://www.partizipation.at/aarhus-convention.html.

59 Harald Heinrichs, "Herausforderung Nachhaltigkeit: Transformation durch Partizipation?," in *Partizipation, Öffentlichkeitsbeteiligung, Nachhaltigkeit: Perspektiven der Politischen Ökonomie*, ed. Peter H. Feindt and Jens Newig (Marburg: Metropolis Verlag, 2005), 43–64.

60 Matthew Ryan and Graham Smith, "Defining Mini-Publics," in *Deliberative MiniPublics: Involving Citizens in the Democratic Process*, ed. Kimmo Grönlund, André Bächtiger, and Maija Setälä (Colchester: ECPR Press, 2014), 9–26.

61 For an overview and definitions of various participation formats, see http://www.participedia.net/.

62 Patrizia Nanz and Miriam Fritsche, *Handbuch Bürgerbeteiligung: Akteure und Verfahren, Chancen und Grenzen* (Bonn: Bundeszentrale für politische Bildung, 2012; 2016).

63 Sophia Alcántara, Nicolas Bach, Rainer Kuhn, and Peter Ullrich, *Demokratietheorie und Partizipationspraxis:*

Analyse und Anwendungspotentialer deliberativer Verfahren (Wiesbaden: Springer, 2015).

64   Gabriel and Kersting, "Partizipation auf kommunaler Ebene."

65   Winfried Thaa, "Die Auseinandersetzungen um 'Stuttgart 21' und die Zukunft der repräsentativen Demokratie," in *Kursbuch Bürgerbeteiligung*, ed. Jörg Sommer (Berlin: Deutsche Umweltstiftung, 2015), 284–306.

66   The German term for this transition, *Energiewende,* refers to a body of intertwined and interdependent legislation and policies aimed at facilitating a transition to an affordable and reliable low-carbon energy system. This long-term energy and climate strategy focuses broadly on developing renewable energy generation capacities and improving energy efficiency.

67   Jan-Hendrik Kamlage, Ina Richter, and Patrizia Nanz, "An den Grenzen der Bürgerbeteiligung: Informelle dialogorientierte Bürgerbeteiligung im Netzausbau der Energiewende," in *Energiewende und Partizipation. Transformationen von Gesellschaft und Technik*, ed. Jörg Radtke and Lars Holstenkamp (Wiesbaden: Springer, 2016); and Pia-Johanna Schweizer and Ortwin Renn, "Partizipation in Technikkontroversen: Panakeia für die Energiewende?," *Technikfolgenabschätzung: Theorie und Praxis* 2, no. 2 (2013): 42–47.

68   Gabriel and Kersting "Partizipation auf kommunaler Ebene."

69   In German the prayer is, "*O heiliger Sankt Florian, verschon' mein Haus, zünd' and're an.*"

70   Klaus Selle, "'Particitainment,' oder: Beteiligen wir uns zu Tode?," in *Über Bürgerbeteiligung hinaus: Stadtteilentwicklung als Gemeinschaftsaufgabe? Analysen und Konzepte* (Detmold: Verlag Dorothea Rohn, 2013), 275–308.

71   Anna Geis, "Das 'Schlichtungsverfahren' zu 'Stuttgart 21': Die neueste demokratische Errungenschaft?," in *Zur kritischen Theorie der politischen Gesellschaft*, ed. Olaf Asbach et al. (Wiesbaden: Springer, 2012), 155.

72   See, for example, Michael Wilk and Bernd Sahler, eds., *Strategische Einbindung: Von Mediationen, Schlichtungen, runden Tischen . . . und wie Protestbewegungen manipuliert werden* (Lich: Edition AV, 2014).

73   *Guidelines for citizen participation in the City of Heidelberg*, adopted 25 July 2012, updated 26 March 2015, http://www.heidelberg.de/.

74   *Weißbuch Konversion und Bürgerbeteiligung in Mannheim,* accessed December 7, 2015, http://www.konversion-mannheim.de/sites/default/files/weissbuch_iii.pdf (site discontinued).

75   *Demoenergie* is a joint undertaking of the Institute for Advanced Studies in the Humanities (KWI) and the Institute for Advanced Sustainability Studies (IASS). The project is funded by the Federal Ministry of Education and Research (BMBF). See http://www.demoenergie.de/.

76   Klaus Selle, "Particitainment."

77   Habermas, *Between Facts and Norms.*

78   Carole Pateman, "Participatory Democracy Revisited," *Perspectives on Politics* 10 (2012): 7–19.

79   Christian Vogel, "Der wahre Egoist kooperiert:
     Ethische Probleme im Bereich von Evolutionsbiologie,
     Verhaltensforschung und Soziobiologie," in *Denken
     unterwegs: Fünfzehn metawissenschaftliche Exkursionen*,
     ed. Heinz-Dieter Ebbinghaus and Gerhard Vollmer
     (Stuttgart: S.Hirzel Wissenschaftliche Verlagsgesellschaft,
     1992), 169–182.

80   Robert Axelrod, *The Evolution of Cooperation,* rev. ed.
     (New York: Basic Books, 2006).

81   Evidence for this can be found in both behavioural
     science and behavioural economics. On the former, see
     Martin Novak and Roger Highfield, *SuperCooperators:
     Altruism, Evolution and Why We Need Each Other to
     Succeed* (New York: Free Press, 2011); on the latter, see
     Dirk Messner, Alejandro Guarín, and Daniel Haun, "The
     Behavioural Dimensions of International Cooperation,"
     Global Cooperation Research Papers 1 (2013), https://
     www.die-gdi.de/. Experiments conducted by Michael To-
     masello and Daniel Haun with chimpanzees and toddlers
     have shown that cooperation is a common practice that
     rewards collaboration by maximizing benefits derived
     from collective action. See Michael Tomasello, *Why We
     Cooperate* (Cambridge, UK: The MIT Press, 2009).

82   Claus Leggewie, "The Concrete Utopia of the Gift," in
     *Global Cooperation and the Human Factor in International
     Relations*, ed. Dirk Messner and Silke Weinlich (Oxford:
     Routledge, 2015), 181–197.

83   Joachim Bauer, *Prinzip Menschlichkeit: Warum wir von
     Natur aus kooperieren* (Hamburg: Hoffmann und Campe,
     2006).

84 See also Evan Thompson, *Mind in Life: Biology, Phenomenology, and the Sciences of Mind* (Cambridge, MA: Harvard University Press, 2007).

85 Martha C. Nussbaum, *Political Emotions: Why Love Matters for Justice* (Cambridge, MA: Harvard University Press, 2015).

86 Sharon R. Krause, *Civil Passions: Moral Sentiment and Democratic Deliberation* (Princeton, NJ: Princeton University Press, 2008).

87 Charles Taylor, *The Malaise of Modernity* (Concord, ON: House of Anansi Press, 1991).

88 Jane J. Mansbridge, *Beyond Adversary Democracy* (Chicago: University of Chicago Press, 1983), 27.

89 Elinor Ostrom, "The Challenge of Common-Pool-Resources," *Environment: Science and Policy for Sustainable Development* 50, no. 4 (2008); Paul D. Aligicia *Rethinking Institutional Analysis: Interviews with Vincent and Elinor Ostrom* (Washington, DC: Mercator Center, George Mason University, 2003).

90 Richard Sennett, *Together: The Rituals, Pleasures and Politics of Cooperation* (New Haven, CT: Yale University Press 2012), 15.

91 Hannah Arendt, "Truth and Politics," in *Truth: Engagement Across Philosophical Traditions*, ed. José Medina and David Wood (Oxford: Blackwell Publishing, 2005), 295-314.

92 Mikhail Bakhtin, *Speech Genres and Other Late Essays* (Austin, TX: University of Texas Press, 1986).

93 Frank Adloff and Claus Leggewie, eds., *Das konvivialistische Manifest: Für eine neue Kunst des Zusammenlebens* (Bielefeld: Transcript Verlag, 2014).

94   Larry Leifer, Hasso Plattner, and Christoph Meinei, eds.,
     Design Thinking Research: Building Innovative Eco-Systems
     (Wiesbaden: Springer 2014); Alex Pentland, "On the
     Collective Nature of Human Intelligence," *Journal of
     Adaptive Behaviour* (June 2007), https://doi.org/10.1177
     %2F1059712307078653.

95   On empathy, see Fritz Breithaupt, *Kulturen der Empathie*
     (Frankfurt: Suhrkamp, 2009); Leslie Jamison, *The Empa-
     thy Exams: Essays* (London: Granta Books, 2015); James
     Tully, "Citizenship for the love of the World," (lecture,
     Cornell University, Ithaca, NY, March 14, 2013); and
     Evan Thompson, *Mind in Life*. On trust, see Martin
     Endreß, *Vertrauen* (Bielefeld: Transcript Verlag, 2015).
     On cooperation, see Sennett, *Together*. In our view,
     cooperation is synonymous with the ethical principle
     of "collaboration," as both processes change the partic-
     ipants. See also Mark Terkessidis, *Kollaboration* (Berlin:
     Suhrkamp, 2015). On our desire for communal relation-
     ships, see Charles Taylor, *Wieviel Gemeinschaft braucht die
     Demokratie?*; and Alison Gopnik, *The Philosophical Baby:
     What Children's Minds Tell Us about Truth, Love, and the
     Meaning of Life* (New York: Picador, 2009).

96   Scott Barrett, *Why Cooperate? The Incentive to Supply
     Global Public Goods* (Oxford: Oxford University Press,
     2010).

97   Wissenschaftlicher Beirat der Bundesregierung Globale
     Umweltveränderungen (WBGU), *Welt im Wandel:
     Gesellschaftsvertrag für eine Große Transformation* (Berlin:
     WGBU, 2011).

98   Andreas Scherbel, "Die Begründung von Generationen-
     gerechtigkeit im Schöpfungsglauben der monotheis-

tischen Offenbarungsreligionen," in *Handbuch Genera-tionengerechtigkeit*, ed. Stiftung für die Rechte zukünftiger Generationen (Munich: Oekom Verlag, 2003), 175–197. The quotation appears on p. 178.

99 As Hannah Arendt writes, "The more people's stand-points I have present in my mind while I am pondering a given issue, and the better I can imagine how I would feel and think if I were in their place, the stronger will be my capacity for representative thinking and the more valid my final conclusions, my opinion." A standpoint is developed, she argues, "through all kinds of conflicting views, until it finally ascends from these particularities to some impartial generality." *Between Past and Future*, rev. ed. (New York: Viking Press, 1968). See also Tom Atlee, *The Manifesto: A Call to Establish a Legitimate, Wise, Powerful, Collective Voice of the People,* http://empower-ingpublicwisdom.us/the-manifesto/.

100 Thomas Haderlapp and Rita Trattnig, *Zukunftsfähigkeit ist eine Frage der Kultur: Hemmnisse, Widersprüche und Gelingensfaktoren des kulturellen Wandels* (Munich: Oe-kom Verlag, 2013), 591.

101 Taylor, *Wieviel Gemeinschaft braucht die Demokratie?*.

102 Participation and Sustainable Development in Europe, http://www.partizipation.at/.

103 For an alternative proposal, in which the tasks of agenda setting and scrutiny are addressed separately, see D. Own and G. Smith, "Sortition, Rotation and Mandate: Condi-tions for Political Equality and Deliberative Reasoning," *Politics and Society* 46, no. 3 (2018): 419-434.

104 While there are some thematic and procedural similarities between the two, these should not be confused with the

future council proposed here. See Nanz and Fritsche, *Handbuch Bürgerbeteiligung*.

105 Claus Leggewie and Patrizia Nanz have longstanding ties with the Institute for Advanced Study in the Humanities (KWI) in Essen, which has, since 2008, initiated and implemented numerous participation projects in its research areas (Climate and Culture and Culture of Participation) with funding from the Mercator Foundation and the Federal Ministry for Research and Education (BMBF). Similarly, the European Institute for Public Participation (EIPP), of which Patrizia Nanz is a founding member, has facilitated and evaluated participatory processes on a continuous basis since 2009.

106 The concept of future-proof decision-making originated in the context of the debate on environmental sustainability, from which most of the examples and evidence in this book are drawn. Future councils are nevertheless well-suited to address other issues such as education, demographic change, digitalization, and similar challenges.

107 Winfried Kretschmann, comment on Facebook, November 11, 2011, https://de-de.facebook.com/WinfriedKretschmann/posts/181998268554407.

108 Ostrom, "Challenge of Common-Pool Resources"; Silke Helfrich and David Bollier, eds., *Die Welt der Commons: Muster gemeinsamen Handelns* (Bielefeld: Transcript Verlag, 2015).

109 "UN Sustainable Development Goals," http://sustainabledevelopment.un.org/. See also Manuel Rivera, "Entpolitisierung im Konsens: Ein kritischer Blick auf die Entstehung der SDG," in *Globale politische Ziele: Be-*

standsaufnahme und Ausblick des Post-2015 Prozesses, ed. Philipp Lepenies and Elena Sondermann (Baden-Baden: Nomos, 2017), 219-246.

110 These are not strictly geographical terms but rather a replacement for the old First World/Third World paradigm, which was rendered obsolete by the disappearance of the so-called Second World at the end of the Cold War.

111 This project, which aims to revitalize a former industrial district while implementing modern energy efficiency and climate protection standards, has been recognized with the National German Sustainability Award. For further information, see the Innovation City Ruhr website: http://www.icruhr.de/.

112 "Büro für Zukunftsfragen: Aufgaben und Leistungen," https://vorarlberg.at/.

113 See, for example, Manfred Sader, *Psychologie der Gruppe* (Weinheim/Munich: Beltz Juventa, 2008), 62ff. The dynamic facilitation method is suitable for groups of between eight and twenty participants. See also "Dynamic Facilitation," Participation and Sustainable Development in Europe, http://www.partizipation.at/dynamic_facilitation_en.html.

114 Hubertus Buchstein, "Lostrommel und Wahlurne: Losverfahren in der parlamentarischen Demokratie," *Zeitschrift für Parlamentsfragen* 4, no. 2 (2013): 384–404; Hubertus Buchstein, "Wählen, Losen und politische Gerechtigkeit: Plädoyer für einen demokratisch-deliberativen pouvoir neutre," *Zeitschrift für Politikwissenschaft* 22, no. 3 (2012): 397–407; and Buchstein, "Die Legitimitätspolitik der Aleatorischen Demokratietheorie,"

in *Der Aufstieg der Legitimitätspolitik: Rechtfertigung und Kritik politisch-ökonomischer Ordnungen*, ed. Anna Geis, Frank Nullmeier, and Christopher Daase (Baden-Baden: Nomos, 2012), 359–376.

115 See, for example, MASS LPB Inc, *How to Run a Civic Lottery: Designing Fair Selection Mechanisms for Deliberative Public Processes, A Guide and* License *(Version 1.4)*, 2017, https://static1.squarespace.com/static/ 55af0533e4b04fd6bca65bc8/t/ 5aafb4b66d2a7312c182b69d/ 1521464506233/Lotto_Paper_v1.1.2.pdf

116 A 2015 survey of youth conducted in Germany showed that while many young people become politically aware at an early age this potential is frequently neglected. Instead, political actors frequently choose to engage with youth through social media as a form of compensation. Mathias Albert et al., *Jugend 2015,* Shell Jugendstudie 17 (Hamburg, October 2015), https://www.shell.de/.

117 See, for example, Elisabetta Nadalutti and Otto Kallschere, eds., *Region-Making and Cross-Border Co-operation: New Evidence from Four Continents* (Oxford: Routledge, 2017); and Alan Renwick et al., *Report of the Citizen's Assembly on Brexit* (London: Constitution Unit, University College London, 2017), http://citizensassembly.co.uk/.

118 Robert A. Dahl, *Democracy and Its Critics* (New Haven, CT: Yale University Press, 1989).

119 On the difference between "standing for" and "acting for," see Hanna Fenichel Pitkin, *The Concept of Representation* (Berkeley, CA: University of California Press, 1967).

120 Hans J. Lietzmann, "Die Kontingenz der Repräsentation: Bürgerbeteiligung," in *Zur kritischen Theorie der politischen Gesellschaft*, ed. Olaf Asbach et al. (Wiesbaden: Springer, 2012), 165–188.

121 See Katrine Grolsh, "Grundbegriffe," updated November 25, 2002, http://eswf.uni-koeln.de/lehre/0203/ws0203/V61.html.

122 Andrew Dobson, *Listening for Democracy: Recognition, Representation, Reconciliation* (Oxford: Oxford University Press, 2014).

123 This is the focus of research conducted by the Hamburg-based research training group Performing Citizenship, for example, which provided us with valuable input.

124 Graham Smith drew our attention to a possible contradiction between the proposed permeability of councils at various levels and the random selection of citizens as the basis for convening future councils. He fears that local citizen activists could undermine the principle of random selection. However, this exception is made on pragmatic grounds. While individual applications to serve on a future council should not be considered as a rule, in cases where no other suitable candidates can be identified, an exception could be made for citizens who have served on a council at a different level of governance. While this risks fostering the emergence of a "participation elite," it would also enable future councils to tap into the experience of citizens who have served on a council at a different level of governance.

125 See Helmut Dubiel, "Integration durch Konflikt?," *Kölner Zeitschrift für Soziologie und Sozialpsychologie* 39 (1999): 132–143.

126 See, for example, the various training opportunities offered by Führungsakademie Baden-Württemberg, https://www.diefuehrungsakademie.de/angebote.

127 Studiengang Planung und Partizipation, Universität Stuttgart, http://www.uni-stuttgart.de/.

128 Christina Baldwin and Ann Linnea, *The Circle Way: A Leader in Every Chair* (San Francisco: Berrett-Koehler Publishers, 2010).

129 For example, "dynamic facilitation." See http://www.partizipation.at/dynamic_facilitation_en.html.

130 Zunkunfts Orte: Plattform der innovativen Gemeinden Österreichs, http://www.zukunftsorte.at/.

131 John R. Parkinson, *Democracy and Public Space: The Physical Sites of Democratic Performance* (New York: Oxford University Press, 2012).

132 Ortwin Renn, email message to the authors, November 28, 2015.

133 Examples of such trials include the multi-generational dialog conducted in 2010 as part of the InnovationCity Ruhr initiative; the Zukunftsrat Ruhr (Ruhr Future Council) as part of the Ruhrtriennale 2015 (through to 2017); and the Bürgerdialog Ruhr (Ruhr Citizens' Dialog) in September and November 2015 within the framework of the research alliance "Energiewende Ruhr." See http://energiewende-ruhr.de/; and Mechthild Baumann, Sandra Felten, and Eckart D. Stratenschulte, *Empirische Auswertung der Europäischen Bürgerforen 2008/2009* (Berlin, 2009), http://www.buergerforen.de/finale_Auswertung.pdf (Password protected).

134 Rüdiger Goldschmidt, Ortwin Renn, and Sonja
    Köppel, *European Citizens' Consultations: Final Evalua-
    tion Report*, Stuttgarter Beiträge zur Risiko- und Nach-
    haltigkeitsforschung, no. 8 (March 2008), http://dx.doi.
    org/10.18419/opus-5491.

135 Raphaël Kies and Patrizia Nanz eds., *Is Europe Listening
    to Us? Successes and Failures of EU Citizen Consultations*
    (Farnham, UK: Routledge, 2013).

136 Graham Smith, "Designing Democratic Innovations at
    the European Level: Lessons from the Experiments," in
    Raphaël Kies and Patrizia Nanz, *Is Europe Listening to
    Us?*, 201–216.

137 Jan-Hendrik Kamlage and Patrizia Nanz, "Krise und
    Partizipation in der Europäischen Union: Für eine neue
    Politik der Bürgerbeteiligung am Beispiel der Ener-
    giepolitik," in *Europa, wie weiter? Perspektiven eines Pro-
    jekts in der Krise*, ed. Winfried Brömmel, Helmut König,
    and Manfred Sicking (Bielefeld: Transcript Verlag, 2015),
    153–176.

138 See, especially, European Commission, *Governance in the
    European Union: A White Paper*, July 25, 2001, https://
    ec.europa.eu/. The white paper makes explicit note of the
    deliberative nature of European decision-making process-
    es and the vital roles of "inclusion and participation" in
    securing legitimacy—aspects of the basic principles that
    have not been substantially implemented to date. See also
    the Treaty of Lisbon (Article 11), http://data.europa.eu/
    eli/treaty/lis/sign.

139 For further information, see http://www.weyarn.de/
   aktiv.htm.
140 Katja Klee, head of the Coordination Office of the
   municipality of Weyarn (Bavaria), interviewed by Patrizia
   Nanz, 3 December 2015.

INDEX